Return Flights
in
War and Peace

To Jean who, like me, endured six years of wartime service and when it was over was the best wife and mother that any man could wish for.

Return Flights in War and Peace

The Flying Memoirs of Squadron Leader John Rowland DSO, DFC*

Pen & Sword
AVIATION

First published in Great Britain in 2011 by
Pen and Sword Aviation
An imprint of
Pen and Sword Books Ltd
47 Church Street
Barnsley
South Yorkshire
S70 2AS

Copyright © John Rowland 2011

ISBN 978 1 84884 407 0

The right of John Rowland to be identified as the author of this work has been asserted by him in accordance with the Copyright, Designs and Patents Act 1988.

A CIP record for this book is available from the British Library

All rights reserved. No part of this book may be reproduced or transmitted in any form or by any means, electronic or mechanical, including photocopying, recording or by any information storage and retrieval system, without permission from the Publisher in writing.

The views and opinions expressed in this book are those of the author and contributors alone, and should not be taken to represent those of HMG, MoD, the RAF or any government agency.

Printed and bound by CPI UK

Pen and Sword Books Ltd incorporates the imprints of Pen and Sword Aviation, Pen and Sword Maritime, Pen and Sword Military, Wharncliffe Local History, Pen and Sword Select, Pen and Sword Military Classics and Leo Cooper.

For a complete list of Pen and Sword titles please contact
PEN AND SWORD BOOKS LIMITED
47 Church Street, Barnsley, South Yorkshire, S70 2AS, England
E-mail: enquiries@pen-and-sword.co.uk
Website: www.pen-and-sword.co.uk

Contents

Acknowledgements 7
1 Early Days 9
2 Cranwell, Pre-war 18
3 Cranwell at War 26
4 Army Co-op 34
5 613 Squadron 41
6 Calais 45
7 Home Defence 55
8 Instructor Course at CFS 60
9 Instructor at Monrose 64
10 Instructor at CFS 71
11 Bomber Command at Hixon OTU 78
12 First Tour in 12 Squadron 91
13 Back at Lindholme 125
14 Second Tour in 625 Squadron 132
15 Seconded to BOAC 151
16 Dakotas 156
17 Crossing Africa 171
18 Haltons 179
19 Yorks 183
20 Grounded 193
Index 209

Acknowledgements

I have to thank Eddie Doig for badgering me unmercifully for many years to write a book, so that in the end I gave in.

I also wish to thank several members of my family for helping me with the computing. In particular, thank you to my eldest son, Michael, for spending many hours putting it all together in the correct order, and my other son, Philip, and grandson, James, for getting it all onto disc.

Many thanks also to David Williams for much information and photographs of the German night fighter pilots and equipment.

Thanks are due also to Ting Baker who edited my manuscript.

Chapter 1

Early Days

One day in May 1939, I boarded the train at Cardiff, then joined the small local train at Newark. I noticed that there were quite a few lads of my age also on board. When we got to Sleaford station, which was the local station for Cranwell, I disembarked and found that all the other young men had got out as well, about thirty of them. We looked askance at each other, wondering what happened next. A man in the uniform of an RAF warrant officer, holding a clipboard, appeared. 'Right you lot. Answer your names when I call them out and get fell in in one rank.' He proceeded to run down the list on his clipboard and as the others heard their names called they lined up as instructed, until there were only two of us left. Getting to Cranwell was, to me, such a dream that I almost believed that when he came to the end of his list I alone would be left uncalled for and he would look at me and say 'And who are you?' But, at length, I heard my name called. 'Rowland,' he said. At that moment I realized that my wildest dream had come true and that I really was going to be a cadet at Cranwell. I had always longed for this but for many years had believed that it would not be possible.

I was born in 1919, and as a result I was in my teens at the time of the Schneider Trophy races. I have been mad about aeroplanes for as long as I can remember so, naturally, I was fascinated by the exploits of the British entries. These were all provided by the RAF and the pilots became my heroes, in particular Flight Lieutenant Waghorn who won the race in 1938. I was devastated to hear a few years later that he had been killed in a flying accident. He had to bale out of a Hawker Horsley that he was testing. He got out of the plane safely but was fatally injured when he landed on the gable of a house.

During the 1930s I did manage to get a few flights. At that time a lot of holiday resorts had a pilot operating an aeroplane from a farmer's field nearby who offered a quick flight around the field for five shillings (25p). And I was dying to have one of these. My chance came in 1935. A man called Alan Cobham formed Alan Cobham's Flying Circus, which toured the country with about ten aircraft with the object of increasing public interest in aviation. There were several other similar organizations. In 1935 I was on holiday with my father in New Quay, Cardiganshire, when it was advertised that the Flying Circus was coming to Aberaeron, about ten miles away. I managed to persuade my father to take us to see it. When we arrived, we found that they were offering a quick flight around the field for five shillings. I suggested that we went up, but my father was not willing to go as he thought it was too dangerous and he would not let me go by myself. But I managed to persuade a gentleman, who had come with us, to risk it. The plane was a small biplane called a Desoutter, which carried the pilot in the front cockpit and two passengers in the back. This enabled the operator to double the flight income to ten shillings. I have a photograph of us beside the plane, taken after we landed by an enterprising gentleman who was doing a roaring trade taking photographs of all who landed.

Later that year I was very lucky. I was at Porthcawl on the Glamorgan coast near Cardiff, where there was a pilot giving trips for five shillings in an Avro 504. He was increasing his takings by towing advertising banners behind his plane past

Early Days

the holidaymakers on the shore. When I arrived with my five shillings, he very sportingly said that he was just about to do one of these advertising flights and I could come along for the same payment. So this time I had the luxury of a fifteen-minute flight. Sheer heaven.

The following year I was in Weston-super-Mare when Alan Cobham's Flying Circus came. He had about ten aeroplanes, including a ten-seater Airspeed Ferry. The Ferry was an aircraft of unusual design. It was a fairly large biplane with three engines, one on each side on the lower wing and the third in the centre on the top wing. It was not commercially successful; Airspeed only built three, and Cobham ordered one mainly to help Airspeed get production going. But the Ferry was useful to his Flying Circus as it carried ten passengers and many enthusiasts had their first flight in it. Every day, he used to fly all his planes past the town in formation to advertise his presence. When I arrived they were just about to make this formation flight and for ten shillings I got a place on this flight in one of the smaller planes. So I was, again, lucky and this time had a flight of about twenty minutes at a bargain price. The plane I was in flew next to the Airspeed Ferry in the formation so I had a good view of it.

I grew up wishing to have a career in flying, which meant the RAF, but my father, who was clerk of the Glamorgan County Council, poured cold water on this idea. He said that in the RAF you had to retire in your forties and what would you do then! I had no answer to this, and as I was very good at maths he used his influence to get me a position at the head office of the Atlas Assurance Company, with the intention of becoming an actuary. And so, in the summer of 1938 I moved into digs in Kingston upon Thames and commenced commuting to the office of the Atlas on Cheapside in the city.

Kingston was a long way from the centre of London, and the commute to work took an hour each way. To get to the office by the necessary nine o'clock I had to get the eight o'clock train from Kingston to Waterloo, after fifteen minutes' walk from the house. This meant getting out of bed no later than seven. When the train came in at Kingston it was already full and I never got a seat; in fact I had a job to find anywhere to stand. On arrival at Waterloo I had to take the one-stop Underground link to the bank. This train was even more crowded than the Southern Electric train. It came to the surface near the Bank of England and I had to walk a quarter of a mile along Cheapside to the head office of the Atlas.

I worked in the life department as the junior office boy, at the beck and call of everybody. My main task every morning was to wait until the post had been opened and scanned. I then went down to the bowels of the building and fetched up whatever copies of records were needed after studying the incoming letters of the morning's post. This job is no longer needed now that everything is done by computer.

A new office boy must have arrived because I was moved to the annuities department, which consisted of me and the boss of the department, Mr Dyas. In those days the insurance industry only paid out annuities when it had been proved that the recipient was still alive. This necessitated sending out a form that had to be signed by a responsible person (doctor, solicitor, policeman etc), to certify that the recipient was still alive on the due date. When this form was received the annuities department authorized the accounts department to make the payment and a cheque was sent out. Today, common sense has intervened and insurance companies pay out on the due day regardless, as they have found out that it is more expensive to send out all the certificates than to get the money back from the estate of the deceased. The executors always send the money back as soon as they find it was not due.

Early Days

This was steady work but it tended to have its ups and downs, as people liked to get their payments on a date that suited them so a lot was due on the first of the month. Also, the number due at Christmas and the new year became very large, as did the amount of work that it was necessary for us to do. The life department was on the top floor and most of the employees like Mr Dyas were ordinary unqualified clerks, without qualifications, earning modest wages. The big earners were the actuaries. The Atlas had three: one who was the head of the life department, one who was the general manager and the third was his deputy. In those days the ordinary unqualified clerks earned in the region of £500 a year, but it was rumoured that the head of the life department was on £3,000 and the other two somewhere up around £10,000. My pay was £60 a year. Each month, I was the recipient of £5, which was not even enough to pay the rent of my lodgings, so I was heavily subsidized by my parents. I comforted myself that as a trainee to be an actuary I would be well up the scale. But I had to go to evening classes one day a week at the Sir John Cass Academy where I found the level of mathematics was becoming a bit of a problem for me.

Every day, the work that had arrived from the branches had to be dealt with if humanly possible and the typists worked at high speed to get it all typed, signed and addressed back to the branches in time to catch the evening post at the post office in the street outside leading to the Mansion House from Cheapside. The Atlas was on the corner and one advantage was that we had a grandstand view of the procession of the Lord Mayor's Show every summer.

I had been getting very fed up with the long journey to work every day when I had a piece of luck. My brother, David, and I had become very friendly with a man called Gordon Nixon-Smith, who happened to work in London in the West End. He was a salesman in a firm that sold cars in

Great Portland Street. He had a wonderful sense of humour and always deprecated his job. He was in the habit of telling acquaintances that he had been ashamed to tell his mother that he was a car salesman in Great Portland Street. He had told her that he was a pianist in a brothel! Anyway, he lived in digs in Streatham, which was quite a lot closer to the city than Richmond and was also on the Underground network with very frequent trains, unlike the Southern Electric where if you missed your train you might have to wait half an hour for another. It happened that there was a spare room in his digs so I moved in and found it a great improvement.

By a strange piece of fate it turned out that working at the Atlas managed to get me into my flying career. Every morning we were brought a coffee at eleven o'clock, and we had a ten-minute break while we chatted among ourselves. One day, one of the young men started talking about going off flying at the weekend. My ears pricked up at hearing this and I soon found out that he had joined the RAF Volunteer Reserve as a pilot. They were the RAF equivalent of the Territorial Army. They taught you how to fly whenever you cared to turn up at the flying school to which you were attached. This meant mainly at the weekend.

After pumping him for the necessary information, I sent off my application to join. A few weeks later I got a reply accepting me, giving me the rank of sergeant and allotting me to a centre in Tottenham Court Road for ground instruction and to the E&RFTS (Elementary and Reserve Flying School) at Redhill for flying. Getting to the ground centre was no problem, but getting to Redhill aerodrome was a bit of a journey. I had to take the train to Redhill, but was then faced with the five miles to the airfield, which I had to walk unless I was able to get a lift. Anyway, on 1 October 1938 I was taken up on my first flight by a Flying Officer Lines in a DH60 Moth for fifteen minutes' air experience. The following Saturday I

Early Days

had my first instructional flight with Squadron Leader Thompson, a procedure that was repeated on the following weekends.

Although it was marvellous to be learning to fly at last, I was a bit disappointed to be flying these crummy old DH Moths, so it was a wonderful surprise to turn up on 11 November and see twelve brand-new Miles Magister trainers lined up on the tarmac. Obviously, it was a sign of the RAF expansion that was now taking place. My instruction then took place in these lovely modern monoplanes.

Having started to fly, my ambition to join the regular RAF blossomed and I decided to tackle my parents about it. At this time, Hitler was making warlike noises and a war was becoming to look more likely. When I spoke to my mother on the phone I therefore pointed out that as I was in the reserve I would be called up and sent off to war with very little training, as in the First World War. So, would it not be sensible to go to Cranwell now and be trained properly? To my amazement she bought that one. She agreed that I could go, but only if I could get a prize cadetship, as all the available family money had been spent sending my elder brother to Oxford. At that time, Cranwell was run like a public school with three terms a year and the cadets were civilians who had to pay £100 per annum plus £100 for uniforms. If a prize cadetship, of which four were awarded each term, was obtained these charges were deleted. There was an entrance exam before each term and the twenty top candidates were accepted.

I was very lucky that Cranwell accepted entries up to nineteen and a half, whereas Woolwich and Sandhurst only took entries up to the age of nineteen. I was just nineteen, so I would only get one shot. However, I had done pretty well in maths at school so I felt pretty confident, but I had left school a year earlier to go to the Atlas so it was decided I should go to a firm of crammers who specialized in getting people into Woolwich and Sandhurst and do some revision from January 1939 to the exam in March.

I was able to do some flying while I was preparing for the exam and had my first solo in a Magister on 14 February 1939.

When the results came out in April, to the pleasure of both my parents and me, I passed in top place. This result was assisted by obtaining 290 out of 300 in the interview and recording the highest mark of any candidate. I attributed this to the fact that in the interview the board were extremely impressed that I had joined the Volunteer Reserve and had a certain amount of flying experience already. I was also the only candidate choosing Higher Maths as the other optional subject.

During the gap between the exam and going to Cranwell, I lived at home in Weston-super-Mare. As I was still in the Volunteer Reserve I was still eligible to fly so I got myself transferred to No. 33 E&RFTS at Whitchurch near Bristol. As a result, I did a lot of flying. I was able to finish my elementary training, fifty hours on Tiger Moths. I also went solo on the service type, the Hawker Hind.

I had one interesting experience during this period. My mother had to go up to Bristol to do some business that would take her an hour or so in the afternoon. I suggested that I drive her up and while she was busy I would go out to Whitchurch and do some flying. She agreed, and we arranged to meet in the café of the Odeon cinema at 4.30 pm.

I drove out to the airport, and reported to my instructor, expecting to be given a little dual and solo lasting about an hour. However, he said 'You can do your first cross-country. Hamble, near Southampton, will be the best place.' This was such exciting news that everything else went out of my mind. I immediately prepared my flight plan, about seventy-five minutes, and started off. I arrived safely and after reporting in asked the airman to refuel me for the return journey. While I was waiting for him to do this, I suddenly remembered my appointment with my mother in Bristol. I looked at my watch and saw it was 3.45 pm. I felt a chill in my stomach as I realized I was in serious trouble. I chased up the airman to refuel me as quickly as he could, then set off for Whitchurch at full throttle. When I got to the Odeon it was nearly six, and my mother was absolutely incandescent, helped probably by the fear that I had had an accident, possible fatal. She never forgave me.

Chapter 2

Cranwell, Pre-war

Anyway, I got my prize cadetship and duly arrived at the RAF College Cranwell at the end of April 1939, the beginning of the summer term. I can honestly say that I was the happiest person in the world at having made it.

My course was made up of thirty cadets: the twenty who had passed the exam; a few from the colonies; and two who had been put down from the previous term after they had received serious concussion while competing in the boxing team against more mature people like Royal Marines, Plymouth Dockyard etc.

The Cranwell building was fabulous. The central block contained all the classrooms, anterooms and the library. Leading off from this were three dormitory wings called A, B and C Squadrons. I was in B Squadron. In front of the main building was a large parade ground where all the big parades were held. Beyond this was a large grass area called the orange where cricket matches were held. As new arrivals, we were given a large amount of drill instruction elsewhere until we were good enough to join the other cadets on the large parade ground.

With the expansion that was going on, the college was full to bursting. The cadets each had a single room with a wash basin, but there were not enough for two of the cadets. This was another case where I suffered from having a surname beginning with a letter near the end of the alphabet. Smith

CRANWELL, PRE-WAR

and I were put together in a large room that had previously been a store room. I did not get a room to myself until the following term. We had a batman between each four cadets whose job it was to see that we were turned out correctly and smartly dressed at eight o'clock each morning for the first parade of the day.

There was a branch of Burberry's on the camp that provided us with our uniforms and one of our first tasks was to get fitted out by them. We wore officers' tunics and trousers but without rings of rank on the sleeves. For everyday use we wore grey flannel trousers, keeping the officer-type trousers for best and big parades.

The commandant of the whole camp, which was huge and comprised many training units for other ranks, including a school for wireless operators, was Air Vice Marshal JEA Baldwin, a fairly elderly officer close to retirement. He had started his military career in the First World War in the cavalry and transferred to the Royal Flying Corps. In those days it was considered that good horsemen made good pilots. He was still a very good horseman and played polo for the RAF. He had managed to get as his PA (personal assistant) Pilot Officer Percy Pickard who was also a very good horseman and played polo for the RAF. He would appear on large parades and we got to know him quite well. Baldwin retired at the end of the term but was brought back almost straight away when the war started and was put in command of 3 Group, flying Wellingtons.

It was not long before Percy Pickard turned up in 3 Group. Here, he had a brilliant career and finished up as a group captain in command of a squadron of Mosquitoes. He was awarded three DSOs and the DFC. He became well known to the public when he starred in the documentary film 'Target for Tonight' as the pilot of the bomber. He was shot down and killed during Operation *Jericho* when he led his squadron to bomb the walls of the prison in Amiens so that many French Resistance fighters could escape. The raid was called for by the Resistance who were expecting to be executed at any moment and preferred the risk of being killed by RAF bombs than the certainty of being shot by the *Gestapo*. The story of this is told in the book *And the Walls Came Tumbling Down* by Jack Fishman. The operation was successful and many prisoners escaped. However, Percy was shot down and killed by an FW190 when he hung about too long to assess the success of the operation. He was a wonderful chap whom I have to add to the long list of friends who were not as lucky as me.

On the first day, we were all interviewed individually by our squadron commanders. Mine was Flight Lieutenant Revell, nicknamed Foxy. I do not know why. I marched in to his office and saluted him as smartly as I knew how to then. He was seated behind his desk and fixed me with a stern look. 'There are three things which I must have. Efficiency, smartness and punctuality.' And he thumped the desk hard as he spoke each word. I was very impressed and have done my best to live up to these ideals as well as I can from then onwards. I do not know about the other two but I can honestly say that I have been an extremely punctual man ever since.

The instruction was half ground subjects, half flying. My father had given me a pearl of wisdom before I left. 'Remember, eyes open, mouth shut.' Bearing this in mind, I did not boast too much about having already done some flying but I had to produce my flying log book.

On inspecting this, my flight commander, Flight Lieutenant Slater, told me that I would get away with a reduced number of hours, depending on my progress.

The elementary tuition was on Avro Tutors, on which we normally did fifty hours. Because of my previous experience,

CRANWELL, PRE-WAR

I was the first of my term to go solo, which I did on 4 May 1939, after two hours and forty-five minutes' dual. This included a test with a different flight commander, Flight Lieutenant Macdonald, an Australian who wore the Australian-type dark blue uniform. In the end, I did twenty-seven hours so that in fact I had the benefit of having my elementary flying training nearly twice, which was of great benefit to me.

My instructor was Pilot Officer Stewart, of whom I cannot speak too highly. We never had a cross word. He was very hard working and conscientious. I remember at the end of one day we landed and as we walked in he said he had done seven hours' dual that day. He was very tired and thought it was too much. He was a bit fed up and not at all pleased. I remember being amazed at what he said, as I could not imagine anyone having too much flying.

Our day was divided into two: half for flying and half for lectures. We did not enthuse about having half of each day devoted to attending lectures; all we wanted to do was fly. But it became clear to us that the subjects taught at the lectures were very necessary for us to master. I remember being very cheesed off at having lectures on meteorology, thinking it was very boring. But I later came to realize that it was a very important subject. Our teacher for aerodynamics and theory of flight was a civilian, Mr AC Kermode, a real gen man who had written books on the subject. I remember him telling us about jet engines, which were in the process of being developed, and saying proudly that the leader in the research was an ex-Cranwell cadet, though he did not give any name or any further details.

It was customary at Cranwell to have an event called 'First Term Boxing'. This was carried out in the gym before a large audience, when the new cadets were sorted out in pairs according to their weight and previous experience. The fights were of three one-minute rounds. The object was to see that you were of a strong character. Nobody cared if you were a skilful boxer; one was expected to put up a good show. I had done a bit of boxing at school, usually as an energetic loser, and was paired up with Flight Cadet Marrs who was about the same size as me. There were a lot of fights to get through so in order to save time we had to wait at the ringside during the previous fight so that one could get straight into the ring after it was over.

The fight before me was between two small cadets of equal energy. They hammered each other without stop for the whole three rounds, until they hardly had the strength to lift their arms, let alone throw a punch. By this time they both had nose bleeds and were covered in blood. They presented such a dreadful sight that I was not looking forward to my own fight, but I was determined to put up a good show.

At length, we entered the ring. 'Seconds out, time.' I shook hands, clenched my right fist, and let fly a haymaker with all my strength. By great luck this connected with his jaw, and he went down. He was counted out and was still unconscious in the dressing room after they carried him away. There was a deathly hush from the audience, but the most astonished person there was me. I was very pleased to get away so lightly though.

Very shortly afterwards, I had a test with the chief flying instructor (CFI), Squadron Leader Boyle, later to become Air Chief Marshal and Chief of the Air Staff. As we climbed away after take-off to get to sufficient altitude for aerobatics, he said to me over the intercom, 'Good fight the other day, Rowland. You're just the chap we'll be looking for next term for the boxing team.' I replied 'Yes sir.' But I did not feel very happy about the prospect. One thing I have to thank Hitler for was that he started his war and the next term was completed with no need of a boxing team.

Cranwell, Pre-war

At most Flying Training Schools (FTS) the pupils were trained either on single-engined service types or on twins. At Cranwell these were the Hawker Hart and the Airspeed Oxford respectively. The cadets flew both, with a term on each, half on one and half on the other, changing over for the next term. It was decided that I would fly the Oxford before the end of the term so that the instructors would have a less busy time at the beginning of the next term when they would have a lot of dual to give to everybody getting soloed on the new types. So on 3 July my instructor, Pilot Officer Stewart, took me out to an Oxford but when we got to it an airman said 'Sorry sir, you can't have this one, it's got a flat tyre.' We therefore went back to the flight office. The flight commander had a chat with the maintenance sergeant who told him that there wasn't another Oxford but there was a spare Hart available. OK, said Slater to us, take him up in that. So that is what happened, and I went solo on the Hart on the same day. By the end of term I had done about ten hours on them.

At Cranwell there was a big emphasis on sport. We had to take part in some type of sporting activity for an hour every day. As a first termer I had to keep a record of the sport I had done every day and show it to the cadet under officer at the end of the week. There was an under officer cadet for each squadron; mine was Flight Cadet Kimpton. As it was the summer term I found it difficult to find a form of sport to do as I did not play cricket or squash. I was a keen rugby player and in the winter would have had no trouble. I resorted to going for long walks with another cadet along Ermine Street, which went past the college. I had a job to convince Kimpton that this was sufficient exercise and the relationship between us was not a happy one.

The following term I got into the college rugby team, but by then the war had started and the college was full of the University Air Squadron pupils. Among these there were several rugby Blues, and among them even two internationals: Geddes who had played for Scotland as full back and Coles, an Oxford Blue who had played as a forward for England. Playing in a team with these two was a real pleasure. I had been in the college team at Cheltenham and as a result Cliff Jones, the Welsh international who worked in my father's office, got me a trial with London Welsh in London when I was working there. I went along to a pick up one Saturday afternoon at their practice ground. I left the field an hour later black and blue from head to tail. I realized that there was a huge gap between adult rugby and the schoolboy type and vowed never to play rugby again. But at Cranwell the type of rugby was halfway between the two and I enjoyed it immensely.

This term was marked by a sad event that brought home to us the dangers of flying. On returning to the mess at midday halfway through the term, we noticed that there was a very quiet atmosphere about and it transpired that two senior term flight cadets had been killed in a collision while practising air firing. To make it worse, one of them was Flight Cadet Senior Under Officer RAG Morgan, the senior cadet. The other one was Flight Cadet Guille, This brought home to us that flying could be a risky business,

In the middle of July the term came to an end, marked by the passing out parade for the senior term. The Sword of Honour was won by Under Officer Cadet Neville Stack. He spent the war in Coastal Command flying Sunderland flying boats. As he told me later, he never saw a submarine. But the long flights over the Atlantic, up to ten hours on the alert on the lookout for a submarine periscope, were exhausting and mind-numbingly tedious. But keeping the U-boats below the surface played a vital part in the battle of the Atlantic, which would have cost us the war if it had not been won.

Cranwell, Pre-war

The salute was taken by Lord Gort VC who had just been promoted to Chief of the Imperial General, Staff CIGS, for which we were suitably impressed. This was followed by the passing out ball, to which I invited my parents. The following day we all dispersed for the summer vacation with the expectation of returning for the new term at the beginning of September. However, this was not to be. The international situation was deteriorating rapidly and war seemed likely so we were all recalled from leave on 30 August and I had my first flight of the new term on 31 August.

Chapter 3

Cranwell at War

On 3 September the war started. We had heard on the wireless that if the Germans did not withdraw from Poland by 11 am we would be at war. Nobody expected that they would, and at 10.55 am everybody unobtrusively started collecting near the air raid shelters, half expecting that at one minute past a cloud of German bombers would appear on the horizon and pound us to ashes. Of course, nothing happened. But what did happen was that shortly afterwards a cloud of about thirty Hawker Harts appeared. The pilots of these then got into our Tutors and flew them all away.

Apparently, the college was to be reorganized as a Flying Training School (FTS) for service-type training only. The expected new entry would not come but would do their elementary flying elsewhere before coming to Cranwell. Their places would be filled by members of the University Air Squadrons who were commissioned as pilot officers. We cadets could no longer be allowed to be civilians, so we were all called up as aircraftmen first class (AC1). As their pay of seven shillings a day was more than the six shillings and sixpence a day we had been getting, we received a rise of sixpence a day (2.5p), and everybody was happy. Our course was reduced to about four months, only flying training and associated subjects were to be retained and we would only be trained on either singles or twins, instead of both. As I had already started on Harts, I continued with them. This was a strange development for me because if that Oxford had not had a flat tyre I would have started on Oxfords and carried on with them. I would have passed out as a twin-engined pilot and would not have been posted to Army Co-op, and my career would have been completely different.

When the university people arrived, they turned out to be a very fine collection of people and, nearly all coming from Oxford and Cambridge, they were a very intelligent bunch. But their ideas on discipline were very different to ours.

One of the facts of life in the RAF is the issuing of DROs (Daily Routine Orders). These give all sorts of information about the day's goings on, and it is everybody's duty to read them every morning and act upon them. It is assumed that everybody has read them and it is no excuse to miss something because you did not know about it. This was considered to be a reasonable way of giving necessary information to everybody, but a few of the university types took umbrage and were in the habit of draping red tape around the notice board, which was not thought very well of by the authorities.

One of the ringleaders was Pilot Officer Frank Waldron. I remember that a few weeks after the war started we were notified in DROs to attend a talk that was to be given at 8 pm by the commander of a Wellington squadron who had carried out a sweep over the North Sea and actually caught sight of the German coast. Laughable to us now, but considered quite daring at that time. We were all in the theatre waiting in our seats at 7.55 pm and on the dot the air vice marshal strode on to the stage to introduce the speaker. When he had been speaking for a few minutes, the doors crashed open with a bang and Waldron and a companion entered, carrying on a loud and animated conversation. Needless to say, they chose to head for two empty seats in the middle of a row a few rows from the front, where all the other seats were occupied.

Getting to them necessitated much noise and movement from those they were disturbing, which brought the proceedings to a halt. By now, the air vice marshal was apoplectic with rage and called out to Waldron 'Who the devil are you?' To which Waldron replied coolly, 'Waldron, who are you?'

Needless to say, we cadets were cringing in our seats with embarrassment, as cadets do not talk back to senior officers in that way. It was no surprise when he left the RAF shortly afterwards. Whether it was at his own wish or because he was pushed I do not know. My brother met him later at Sandhurst on the way to a commission in the Scots Guards. I wonder what he thought of the discipline at Sandhurst and in the Guards?

Flying was carried out at a much faster rate so that by 9 November I had completed the necessary fifty hours and was given my wings test, again by Squadron Leader Boyle. When I inspected my log book a few days later I was astonished to see that I had been assessed as 'Exceptional', a great honour.

It was about now that a real step forward in flying technology appeared. It was called the Link Trainer. It was invented and developed by someone who deserves great credit but who receives little. He was an American called Sperry and the business he founded became a huge worldwide corporation. His work revolutionized instrument flying and made it possible to fly safely in any conditions of weather or time of day. He developed the gyroscope, or gyro as it became called. Until then, the gyroscope was regarded as a toy that was able to maintain its position and balance wherever it was put to stand. Until then, all aircraft flying instruments were susceptible to acceleration forces, except the airspeed indicator and the turn and bank. The compass and direction and the fore and aft indicators could not be relied on. But the directional gyro always showed the correct heading whatever happened.

The powers that be in the RAF made a wonderful decision. They developed the standard blind flying panel, which contained the artificial horizon, the directional gyro and all the other flying instruments, and put it in the cockpit of every plane that was built from then on. This meant that whatever plane a pilot climbed into, he was faced with the same standard of instruments that he was used to. As well as the gyroscopic instruments, it contained the airspeed indicator (ASI), the turn and bank, altimeter, rate of climb and dive meter. This panel was also installed in the Link Trainer. There was also a link from it to a cursor that travelled about on a table, which tracked the path that the aircraft would have been flown. This could be placed on a map of a suitable scale and so could be used for cross-country flights by instruments. It was even possible, by using a chart and putting a wind strength into a machine, to do a cross-country flight with a navigator who sat at the chart.

Hours at the Link Trainer now became a compulsory part of a pilot's training. At Cranwell the twin-engined trainer was the Airspeed Oxford, which was a modern aircraft and so had the standard flying panel. But the Harts were fairly obsolete and had been built before the advent of the gyro, as had the Tutor, so they both had very poor sets of flying instruments and were not much good for teaching instrument flying. However, the Tutors were fitted with a hood that could be raised over the rear cockpit so that the pupil could practise a little instrument flying while the instructor in the front cockpit had a perfect view to operate as a safety pilot.

We were then transferred to the Advanced Training Squadron for practical instruction in air gunnery and bombing. Unfortunately, here I put up a couple of blacks.

On 22 November I was sent on a cross-country to Upwood and back with Flight Cadet Rothwell in the rear seat as navigator. We set course to return to Cranwell but as we got near it became very hazy and the visibility dropped to about a half a mile. Despite a good search, we could not find base. I was getting a bit worried about where we were going to get down, when by chance I noticed some very large aircraft in a large field below so I landed amongst them. On arrival, we discovered that we were on Doncaster race course, and the aircraft were the assorted airliners of Imperial Airways, which had been dispersed there.

We rang Cranwell and as it was late we had to stay the night. The next day the weather had cleared so we flew back there to a rather frosty reception from the squadron commander. Of course, as pilot I received the blame, which I thought a bit unfair as Rothwell was the navigator and I only did what he told me.

The very next day, 24 November, in the mid-afternoon I was sent off on a battle flight to 15,000 feet, with Flight Cadet Lecky in the back seat. I foolishly omitted to keep track of my position so that when we came down I had no idea where we were. Unfortunately, we had no maps on board to help me. As it was getting rather late I was worried about being left up in the dark. So when I saw a Miles Magister flying along, I assumed that it knew where it was going and would lead me to an aerodrome. I therefore began to follow him. He kept on a straight northerly course, which took us across the Humber until we came to RAF Leconfield, where we landed. It was nearly dark so we had to spend the night and after notifying base we were ushered off to the officers' mess.

On returning to Cranwell the next day, I received an even frostier reception, and, of course, had nobody but myself to blame this time. So my reputation became a little tarnished.

It was in December that my course had its first fatality, Flight Cadet Smith, the chap who had shared a room with me on my first term. On 13 December we were doing our first night circuits and landings. I flew that night and remember that it was a bit of a hairy experience. It was a rather dark night and we flew from a gooseneck flare path on the North Aerodrome. I had done night dual on a couple of occasions in October and November with Pilot Officer Stewart and Flight Lieutenant Slater but had not gone solo. The Hart was a deathtrap at night if it was too dark to have a horizon, as it had no gyro flying instruments at all, only a turn and bank. Anyway, I managed to do my three circuits and landings after having a few duals with Flight Lieutenant Solbe, after which I went off to bed. But on getting up in the morning I heard that Smith had crashed and become the first of our fatalities.

Little did we know that only seven of us would survive the war. This is a very sad fact as I can honestly say that I have never come across a finer bunch of people. I cannot remember any form of animosity between any of us. I was on good terms with every single one of them, but my particular friend was Flight Cadet Bob Mundy, who had passed in sixteenth place in the entrance exam. One of the first things we had been taught at drill was the right way to salute, which was straight up and down in the RAF. We noticed the different ways in which a salute could be given – the navy way, the American way etc and others. Every service seemed to have its own method of saluting and when it should be carried out. We never saluted without a cap, or headdress as it was better known, but Americans seemed to salute at any excuse. Bob and I were tickled by the American salute and got in the habit of giving each other an exaggerated version when we met; in fact, also several times in between whenever we could find an excuse. I have a photograph of him giving me a salute, greeted as always by a good laugh.

Owing to the speeding up of the training program, the terms senior to us were leaving one after the other until we were the only course left. More university people were coming in to take their place. As a result, the anterooms we occupied became fewer until we were only using the end small one.

I had bought a camera and devised a system to take flash pictures. There was a type of Verey light cartridge called Smoke Puff that the Oxfords used during simulated bombing practice to indicate their position when the bombs would have been released. I discovered that this also gave a good flash and I managed to take some quite good photos by turning off the anteroom lights and throwing a small amount of the magnesium powder, which filled the Verey light cartridge, wrapped in paper, on to the fire. When the paper burned, it ignited the powder and took quite a good picture, despite a small amount of smoke. This gave me an idea to play a practical joke on the university types in the large anteroom. I took a rolled up newspaper containing the powder from a whole cartridge, and went into their room for a friendly chat. I stood with my back to the fire holding the paper in my hands behind me. After about five minutes' cheerful conversation I tossed the paper on to the fire, said 'Well I must be off' and made a hasty exit. I waited for a few minutes, then there was a small bang and their anteroom filled with smoke, causing them all to rush out for some fresh air. It was very satisfactory and they never discovered how it was done or who did it.

By the end of January we had finished our flying training and only had to do a few weeks at the armament camp at West Freugh in Scotland near Stranraer where the firing ranges were. I went up by train with a few others and waited for the rest to fly up shortly afterwards. I went into town for the evening one day by bus, and at midnight went to the bus stop for the return journey. By then it had started to snow. It soon appeared that the bus was not going to come. There were about twenty of our airmen also waiting. Eventually, seeing me in my officers' uniform, they came up to me and said, 'What are you going to do about it?' So I went to the police station and passed the problem on to them. There was a squadron leader on the staff who lived out in the town so the police went and roused him out. Then with the powers available for billeting, they went around the town. They knocked on doors and at each house pushed in an airman saying 'This one is staying here, provide him with food and lodging till further notice.' As an officer I was billeted in the best hotel, which was very acceptable as I wasn't going to pay the bill. I found out later that there were several very happy ladies living on their own who had to endure airmen billeted on them.

When we woke the next morning we found that two feet of snow had fallen and the camp was cut off by drifts on the road that were up to ten foot thick. We did not get back to the camp for a week and as the aircraft were covered in snow and not able to be flown, we could not do anything so we all went back to Cranwell where we were all sent home on indefinite leave as the whole country was covered by a foot of snow.

We were called back on 27 February and did a bit of flying. We were then told that the armament camp was cancelled and we would be commissioned straight away. We were finally commissioned on 6 March 1940. We were anxiously awaiting our postings. Those of us who had been trained on singles were hoping to be posted on fighters but only two of us went there, including Howard-Williams, whose father was an air commodore: he had been prophesying all along that he would go to No. 19 fighter squadron, and he did. P/O Marrs, the chap I had beaten at boxing, was also posted on fighters. The rest of us were divided between Army Co-op and light bombers, Fairey Battles. I was posted with ten others to Old Sarum, the School of Army Co-operation, and we were sent off on leave to report there on 18 March.

Chapter 4

Army Co-op

After my week's leave I reported to the School of Army Co-operation at Old Sarum, just north of Salisbury, driving the two-seater Austin Seven that I had just bought for £15. I met my fellow pupils, who included a good slice of ex-cadets from my course at Cranwell.

We discovered that as well as Lysanders there were Hawker Hectors, Army Co-operation variants of the Hawker Hart but with a Napier Dagger engine instead of the Kestrel that we were used to. This was a larger and heavier engine, which made the Hector a bit nose-heavy but improved the performance a little. These were not up to squadron use but quite adequate for training and, after the Harts, were quite fun to fly.

The Hawker Hector was the seventh and last member of the family of aircraft that had originated with the Hawker Hart light bomber of 1930. It was designed to replace the Hawker Audax as an Army Co-operation aircraft. The most significant change made to the Hector was the replacement of the Rolls-Royce Kestrel engine used in the Audax with a Napier Dagger III engine. The Dagger was too large to fit in the elegant pointed nose of the Hart family, and so the Hector received a more rounded nose. In order to balance the extra weight of the Dagger, the swept-back upper wing of the earlier aircraft was replaced by one with a straight wing.

Army Co-op

Despite these visual changes, the Hector was very similar to the Audax. As a result, development and production were rapid. The first production aircraft made its maiden flight on 14 February 1936. Hawker received orders for 178 Hectors, and despite the production switching from Hawker to Westland, all 178 were complete by the end of 1937.

The Hector equipped seven RAF Army Co-operation squadrons from 1937 to 1938/9, when it was replaced by the Westland Lysander. The Hectors were then transferred to five squadrons of the Auxiliary Air Force (Nos 602, 612, 613, 614 and 615). Of these squadrons, only No. 613 used the Hector operationally. In May 1940 the squadron used its Hectors in attacks on the German troops advancing through northern France, losing two aircraft during one mission near Calais. In June 1940, the squadron finished converting to the Lysander, ending the front-line career of the Hector. Between 1940 and 1942, the Hector served as a glider tug, before more modern aircraft became available for that role.

But the Lysanders, well, the less said the better! Unlike the Hectors, which were adapted bombers, the Lysanders were designed for the job. They were high-wing monoplanes so that one had a perfect view of the ground below, unobstructed by a lower wing. They had a complete set of wing flaps, which enabled them to fly very slowly without stalling and thus could land in a very short space. They did at least have one improvement and that was a two-speed propeller – fine and coarse. Fine was used for take-off and landing, the coarse at all other times. It was an improvement but not a patch on the constant-speed propeller that came in to use later and which was an absolute dream. It also didn't look as if they would be much good if they came up against any Messerschmitts. This later turned out to be only too true. When we found that all we were going to fly, after our hopes of Spitfires and Hurricanes, were these two old hacks, we were not very pleased, not to mention the duties that we were going to carry out in them.

We were told that we were to crew up with a rear gunner, of which there arrived a sufficient number to give one to every pilot on the course. They were nearly all other ranks, some LACs (leading aircraftsmen), others were corporals, but two of them were commissioned, Pilot Officers Houghton and Marsh. Houghton had done a bit of civil flying in light planes so he had a flying helmet made out of some striped material, so he got the name of Tiger. Marcus Marsh was a well known race horse trainer. I was lucky enough to get Tiger as my gunner, which was very pleasant for me as he became a great friend of mine. A couple of years later he was able to get to go on a flying instructors' course and finished the war instructing on elementary types. Marcus Marsh was a little older than the rest of us. In the 1931 season he started with only four horses in his yard. However, one of these was the future Derby winner, Windsor Lad, purchased by Marsh on behalf of the Maharaja of Rajpipla. Windsor Lad moved with Marsh to Lambourn where Charles Smirke was engaged to ride him for the Derby. Marcus Marsh joined the RAF for the war, most of which he spent interned in *Stalag Luft* III after his plane was shot down over Holland. After the war he resumed training.

We had been used to quarter-inch to one mile maps up to now but here we had to get used to one inch to the mile. This was so that one could give accurate map references to the soldiers. For this exercise we had to look for the many dew ponds that dotted the countryside in those parts in the hundreds. But the thing that got up our noses was being taken out into the countryside for TEWTS (tactical exercises without troops), which consisted of having to describe how one would command a small unit to attack an objective that was pointed out to us; definitely not what I joined the RAF to do.

Army Co-op

There was one pleasant aspect of the course. We were trained in gas spraying. We were not expecting our side to use poison gas, but we had to be trained to use it in retaliation if the Germans did. The object was to spray the gas on a column of troops moving along a road. This had to be done at a very low height, about 200 feet. One had to fly alongside the troops, slightly up wind of them so that by the time the gas reached ground level it covered the target. The trouble was that flying slowly along a column of troops at low level was rather dangerous as their guns could easily pick you off. The only way was to take them by surprise, which meant approaching them at ground level, climbing up to 200 feet and spraying them before they had a chance to retaliate, they not having seen or heard you coming. But it is very difficult to navigate at ground level as you cannot see very far. By the time you see your target, if you have not got it right it is too late to turn on to it and to your horror you find you have passed it to one side. Thus it needed a lot of practice, and this in effect gave us impunity to fly low anywhere over Salisbury plain and the surrounding area. If you were caught flying low you could always claim to have got lost!

One of the obstacles to flying really low was telephone wires. In those days the telephone wires were strung between telephone poles in large numbers, possibly 100 to a pole, each one attached to its own insulator on cross bars to keep them separate. These were usually on busy main roads but there were less busy roads that did not have them. One such was the road that went past Stonehenge.

I remember flying low over Amesbury and following the road up the hill to Stonehenge. There was a car approaching me. I was right on the deck and must have presented an alarming prospect. I saw him jam on his brakes, skid and fall into the ditch at the side of the road. I flew on laughing, with him no doubt shaking his fist at me. I remember several times touching my wheels on the surface of the road, where there were no telephones of course. Needless to say, we never had to spray any gas but it was very good fun learning how to do it.

Another activity that we were taught was aerial photography. This was done in two ways, either vertical or oblique. The vertical photographs were taken by a camera fitted pointing straight down from the fuselage. This was used for making maps and for intelligence. The photographs had to be overlapped so that they could be used in pairs on a stereoscope on which the pictures became three dimensional and much more correctly interpreted. The oblique photographs were done by cameras mounted at an angle and very easily taken in a Lysander where the visibility was very good so that the target could be seen at the moment of exposure. But, in the Hector it was very difficult as at that exact moment the target was obscured by the tip of the bottom wing!

I had a bit of bad luck just before the course finished. I went into Salisbury for a night out with Tiger. We both took our own cars. He had an Austin Seven similar to mine and, having had a few drinks, we decided to have a race on the way back to camp. The cars were fitted with shades on the headlights in accordance with the blackout regulations. The headlights on an Austin Seven were very poor in any case, and, with the shades on, the forward visibility was very poor. I was travelling flat out, at about 60 miles per hour, when we approached a slight curve on the final straight leading up to the camp. I did not see it until it was too late and put the wheel over too heavily so that I went into a slide and rolled over sideways, coming to a stop broadside to the road. The car was not very badly damaged and we were able to right it and drive on home. I was not badly injured but I had a bad scrape on the outside of my right knuckle. This was very sore and bled a little so I took it to the doctor in the morning. He cleaned it up and bandaged it up.

When I reported to the CFI at the hangar, Squadron Leader Lee, he looked at the bandage and expressed doubt that my hand was well enough for me to fly. He handed me a broom handle and said 'Grab hold of that.' When I did so he pulled it sharply but I was able to keep hold of it. Nevertheless, he still said that I was not fit to fly and, despite my protestations to the contrary, he kept to his decision. This was a bit awkward as the final test on the course was for Army units to carry out a field exercise and we had to fly over them and after reconnaissance drop reports of our observations to the headquarters in a little weighted bag from a height of about 50 feet. In the end, he decided that I should go in the rear cockpit of a Hector flown by one of the other pilots on the course. This we did and the exercise was satisfactorily completed. I was happy when I found in my log book an assessment as 'Above Average' as an Army Co-operation pilot.

After my accident my Austin Seven was a write-off and I was left without a car, but I was able to remedy this by buying a lovely Alvis open four-seater for £25 from Pilot Officer Tudge, another officer on the course. Unfortunately, the canvas hood was rotten so it was not too good in the rain, but it was a beautiful summer and things were not too bad. And I ran it for several months.

Old Sarum was also host to an Army Co-operation squadron, No. 1 Canadian Squadron, equipped with Lysanders. One of the men was wearing the ribbon of the Jubilee Medal, which I recognized because my father had also received it. The ribbon looked very lonely on his tunic below his wings. One day we received a visit from Air Marshal Trenchard, the founder of the RAF. On his tunic he had about six full rows of medal ribbons. I was having my lunch seated at one of the tables on the opposite side to the single-medalled Canadian when Trenchard walked in. As he walked down the dining room, the Canadian saw him passing. His jaw dropped, then he announced as he looked down at his own medal ribbon, 'Well, out of the tiny acorn the mighty oak may grow.'

We finished our course on 26 April 1940 and awaited our postings to a squadron. But none were forthcoming. Apparently, all the squadrons in France were full and had no vacancies for pilots. This was very disappointing as we had been looking forward to loads of champagne at half a crown (12p) a bottle and lots of amorous and willing young ladies! So, the whole course was posted to Andover to create a pool of pilots. There were no aeroplanes and absolutely nothing to do. The first morning we paraded at eight o'clock and were told to go for a route march around the aerodrome. After lunch we were to hang around the mess. After a week of this we were fed up to the back teeth, so when we paraded the next day and two volunteers were asked for to go to 613 Squadron, at RAF Odiham near Aldershot, my friend ex-cadet John Sowrey and I stepped smartly forward and were accepted.

Chapter 5

613 Squadron

It transpired that No. 613 Squadron was the City of Manchester Auxiliary Squadron, which had been formed only just before the war started, and so had not had time to train any of its own pilots. It was still not fully equipped with Lysanders; half of its planes were still Hectors.

Still, they had aircraft and we had got away from Andover so we were content. There was only one auxiliary pilot in the squadron. The rest of us were either regulars or Volunteer Reservists. As a regular, so the joke went, I was a regular bastard and not a temporary bastard. Auxiliaries wore a little brass A on both lapels of their tunics, Volunteer Reservists wore a brass VR, but regulars had bare lapels. One could therefore distinguish the different classes. After the war started there were no more Short Service Commissions; all new officers were commissioned into the RAF Volunteer Reserve. There also were no new auxiliaries, so as the war progressed nearly all officers were wearing the VR letters on their uniforms. There were no sergeant pilots in Army Co-operation squadrons. I have never been able to find out why, but my opinion is that they were not wanted by the Army, who did not care to have reports brought to them by NCOs, preferring to deal with officers and believing they would be more able to trust their reconnaissance reports. In addition, Army Co-operation squadrons had a few Army officers who had been seconded for a period and taught to fly. One of these was the Commanding Officer, Squadron Leader Anderson, who doubled as a major in the Warwickshire Regiment, though in the event he stayed in the RAF until the end of the war. He finished up as a group captain. This type of officer sometimes continued to wear their Army uniforms but Anderson wore RAF blue, and had been out in France in a Lysander squadron until recently.

I was put in C Flight, but John Sowrey went elsewhere so I did not see so much of him from then on. My flight commander was Flight Lieutenant Gus Weston. He was a retired short service officer who had retired before the war but had been brought back to the colours at the outbreak of hostilities. He was what we thought was a bit elderly, about thirty-five years old I should think, but a cheerful old buffer who was very popular with us youngsters – all about twenty-one.

Because there were so few auxiliary pilots available, all the pilots brought in to bring the squadron up to strength, apart from the flight commanders, were pilot officers. One of them in my flight was a Canadian, Pilot Officer Al Edy. He was a very outgoing person and modesty was not his middle name, but he was quite a likeable chap. He was in a bit of trouble with the CO at the time because he had been overspending his pay and got into debt. This was not allowed in the RAF and he had been confined to the mess and forbidden to patronize the bar until he was solvent again. His debts were not large and he was living for the day in the near future when he would be able to resume the good life. Another was Pilot Officer Stewart, who like all young RAF pilots was full of life and get up and go. He took me up in a Hector on 7 May to show me the local landmarks.

Because Tiger Houghton and I had been regarded as a crew he had come with me to 613 Squadron. His arrival caused quite a stir as he was the first commissioned gunner, and moves were made to gradually pinch him from me. This was never completely successful, although I was sometimes obliged to fly with someone else. Marcus Marsh did not come to 613 Squadron but went to one of the Army Co-op squadrons in France and was shot down and taken prisoner.

It was at this time that there was an unexpected and monumental bombshell. Up until then all the air gunners except for the commissioned ones had been leading aircraftsmen or below in rank, but out of the blue it was announced that all air gunners in future would be sergeants. I believe that because there was a war on it was considered that with the increased risk to aircrew they deserved better pay and conditions. This caused consternation in the sergeants' messes where court had been kept by senior sergeants and warrant officers who had only achieved their rank after many years of arduous service. Their feelings when people who the previous day had been AC1s with a few months' service were walking into the sergeants' mess for a comfortable life, had to be seen to be believed. But they soon became used to it and, eventually, with the advent of larger aircraft with bigger crews, the aircrew sergeants far outnumbered the others.

When I did not fly with Tiger Houghton I flew with LAC Conacher. LAC Conacher was a very likeable Scot who eventually became my regular companion. On 7 June I flew with LAC Conacher and on 11 June I flew with a very happy Sergeant Conacher.

In early June we did a few practice dive-bombing sorties but were not very accurate. Then on 10 June I flew down to Weston-super-Mare with Tiger in the back to have lunch with my family. I introduced him to them and they were very impressed and pleased that I had such a nice-looking chap to look after me. We had a nice walk along the prom where we had a photograph of the two of us taken by Jacksons Faces who made a good living taking pictures of holidaymakers, though business had dropped off with the war.

There was not a lot to do so I was able to arrange a week's leave. But before I left the news broke that the Germans had invaded Holland, so all leave was cancelled.

Chapter 6

Calais

We had no news of what was happening other than what was printed in the press, but the general impression was that things were not going very well.

It became known that all the pilots in the pool had been sent to France and very little was ever heard of them again. Pilot Officer Plumb, one of our ex-cadets, was given a Lysander and told to fly to Lille in France. Unfortunately, he arrived in the circuit at the same time as a Messerschmitt 109 and was shot down and killed, which was a shock to us as he had been very popular. He had been an apprentice at Halton and when he passed out top of his class he was awarded a free cadetship at Cranwell. What a waste to fall so soon after two years' training. Unfortunately, he was only the first of many of my term who became casualties as the war hotted up. Chandler went on to Defiant two-seater fighters and was killed in the Battle of Britain, as was Marrs who I had boxed with. My greatest sadness was to hear that Bob Mundy had been killed in a flying accident, night flying in a Beaufort at Abbotsinch, We had kept in touch by post after we left Cranwell.

One of the tasks of Army Co-op was artillery spotting, that is, observing the fall of shot and communicating with the gunners by WT (wireless) so that they could correct their following shots until they made a hit. We used a clock face to give the direction of the error and a code to give the distance, starting with W for 25 yards, Z for 50, A for 100 and so on. On 14 May I was sent off to Knighton Down, a landing ground on Salisbury Plain on the Larkhill range, to do a week's live shoots. The field adjoined the Army mess where we stayed.

One day, I was observing a shoot when I saw that the first round landed about a thousand yards away from the target. There was a letter for a thousand but because the shot was so far out it was difficult to give a correct direction as the shot did not coincide with any figure. But I remembered that one could add S to the number to denote half past on the clock. So I sent down K8S, which meant 8.30 at a thousand yards. I anxiously awaited the fall of the next shot, and to my amazement the next one landed about fifty yards from the target.

When I landed to discuss the shoot with the gunners, the CO of the artillery school, a brigadier, rushed up and gave me a great hug after I had got out. Apparently, in the mess the previous evening all the pupils had been saying that the code for half past should be scrapped because it would never be of any use, but the brigadier strongly opposed this view on the grounds that there were occasions when it could. So they agreed that the following day they would put a very large error on the first round and see what happened. So he was highly pleased that he had been proved right.

We had no news of what was happening in France except for what was published in the press, but it seemed as if things were not going too well for us. We heard rumours that the Lysander squadrons in France were not doing very well. In fact, they were being shot down in large numbers but as we were equipped partly with Hectors we did not think that there would be any call for us. At length, on 25 May came the news that six Hectors were to proceed to Hawkinge in Kent the following morning at dawn, 4 am, for operational duties.

Calais

I was not among those selected to go but Squadron Leader Anderson set off at dawn accompanied by Pilot Officers Bernard Brown, the New Zealander, Al Edy, Paddy Barthropp, Stewart and Gore. When they arrived they had a long briefing by Air Chief Marshal Sir Edgar Ludlow Hewitt and were astonished to hear that the British Expeditionary Force was in a state of collapse, and that they were to be sent off on a ground-strafing operation to relieve the pressure on the garrison that was holding out in Calais and blocking the Germans from advancing up the coast towards Dunkirk and encircling our troops. It is hard to believe now that such antiquated aircraft should even have been considered for a task like this, but it does demonstrate the desperate state that things were coming to. The weather was fine with no cloud and the aircraft took off at 09.50 hours, each armed with two 100-pound bombs and a Vickers gun firing through the airscrew for the pilot and a Vickers GO gun for the gunner.

The orders were to bomb gun positions outside Calais. Things did not go too well at first as one of Stewart's bombs fell off. However, he carried on with the other one and arrived at Calais at 4,000 feet. He was able to locate one of the gun positions despite the heavy flak that came up at them. He carried out a dive-bombing attack down to 900 feet, scoring a near miss on one of the gun positions, then climbing back through the flak and returning to Hawkinge. Stewart was not the only one to have trouble.

Bernard Brown decided to test his gun over the Channel – a wise precaution as it turned out. After a few rounds he heard a loud explosion and he found himself being sprayed by a jet of petrol that blinded him. It seems that something on the gun had come loose and made a large hole in the main fuel tank, which was in the centre section of the fuselage. Despite being blinded and drenched by the petrol, he was able to maintain control, though it was lucky that there was no fire or he probably would not have survived. After a short time the fuel tank was empty and the spray of petrol came to an end. There was a relief fuel tank in the centre section of the upper wing that operated by gravity and he was able to carry on normal flight. However, by now he was too far away from his objective and had insufficient fuel left so he had to return to Hawkinge.

But he was not the only one to run in to trouble. When Paddy Barthropp dropped his bombs one of them hung up, and the other one was hanging on nose down. This was not his only trouble because as he approached Calais he was fired at by a Royal Navy destroyer. Fortunately their aim was not too good and he escaped unscathed. But the bomb hanging by one fastening presented him with a problem. He did his best to shake the bomb away but it refused to go. So, should he bale out over England after setting the plane on a course for the Channel, or risk landing back at Hawkinge and risk an explosion? He decided to take the risk and he managed to get down safely. As he said to me later, 'I did the smoothest landing of my career.' When they were all back at Hawkinge they were stood down for the day so they returned to Odiham, where they arrived late at night, very tired after a long day and a very early start. On their return their exploits were recounted to the rest of us and we wondered if there would be a repeat the next day.

On his return, Squadron Leader Anderson submitted the following report:

> Six Hector aircraft loaded with 2 x 120 pound bombs, each took off under command of Squadron Leader R F Anderson at 09.50 hrs from Hawkinge. Flight was arranged in two flights of three. No. 1 section under Squadron Leader Anderson, approached the target, carried out high dive bombing attacks combined with front gun attacks, dropping bombs in a salvo. No. 2

section, under Pilot Officer Gore, approached target from the East, from the smoke haze hanging over Calais carrying out similar attacks. All aircraft withdrew independently and returned safely. I saw bursts from my bombs, one dropping within the coppice detailed as the target and one in the open country 450 feet South of it. Gun positions were difficult to identify owing to camouflage but in my opinion guns were in the open. South of the coppice.

Heavy AA fire encountered by No. 2 section and lighter intensity by No. 1 section. Fire apparently consisted of Bofors, heavy AA and light machine gun (tracer). No casualties were sustained by the formation.

But the next day, the orders were repeated and so at 4 am on 27 May I was at the controls of Hector K8108 as we set off for Hawkinge. This was for me to be my baptism of fire and I must admit that I felt a little apprehensive but bolstered my hopes by realizing that all had returned safely the previous day. The planes were piloted by Squadron Leader Anderson, Flight Lieutenant Gus Weston, and Pilot Officers Edy, Jenkyn, Stewart and me. Tiger Houghton had flown with Al Edy the previous day and Gus Weston pinched him again so I had Sergeant Conacher guarding my tail.

On arrival at Hawkinge we found an aerodrome teeming with activity. One memory is of watching a flight of Hurricanes take off in echelon right formation. Unfortunately, although he himself and the next four planes had a clear run, the leader had not left a big enough gap for all the flight to pass and the sixth Hurricane flew slap into a Blenheim parked further over, with dreadful results. There were several Lysanders from the other squadrons, many of them looking to be in a bad state. I remember seeing an airman going up to one when it landed. There was nobody visible in the rear cockpit, so he climbed up and looked inside. He took one look, came down and vomited on the grass.

We proceeded to the ops room where we were taken to look at a large map of northern France. A small area had been marked off around Dunkirk and Calais. This was the Brtish Expeditionary Force (BEF), we were told. We were astonished, as we had no idea that things were anything like as bad as that.

We were told that there was an Army unit holding out in the citadel in Calais but they were running out of ammunition, and could not hold out much longer. It was vital that they should be able to hold on as they were preventing the German Army from advancing up the coast to finish off the British.

It was proposed, therefore, to drop supply containers to them from some Lysanders, which would fly over the citadel at 100 feet while our Hectors flew around the outskirts of the town, two minutes before the drop, to divert attention from the Lysanders so that they could carry out their task without too much interference.

Our task was to fly three Hectors each side of Calais and create as much of a diversion as we could by dropping our bombs and firing our guns at anything we could see. We were also told that we were to act as an escort for the Lysanders, but what use we would be against any Messerschmitt 109s that turned up I do not know. Fortunately, no enemy fighters did turn up, but a myth has built up since that several did turn up and there were scenes reminiscent of a dogfight in the First World War.

The armament of the Hector was a 120-pound bomb under each wing and a Vickers gun firing through the propeller, with the breech in the cockpit on the left side. The Vickers gun was the same model the Army had used since the First World War but it did not need a water jacket to cool it as the barrel was in the slipstream. It had a crank on the right side that moved back and forth as each round was fired, drawing the round out of the breech and pushing another one forward in its place. It was subject to four types of stoppage, numbers one to four, each with the crank in a different position. A number one stoppage was when the round had not quite gone fully in to the breech and it was cured by a slight tap on the crank with a rubber mallet, which was hung in the cockpit. This tap put the round fully in the breech and the gun would then fire when the trigger was pressed. A number three stoppage was with the crank partway back. It was cleared by pulling the crank back by the handle and letting go. Other positions of the crank required different actions, which I regret I cannot remember. But I think I am one of very few people alive who have fired a Vickers machine gun in action from an RAF aircraft through the prop.

The gunner in the rear cockpit had a Vickers GO gun mounted on a Scarff ring, which he was able to aim at any target. He was standing up, and so was not strapped in to a seat like the pilot. He had to have some sort of safety device to stop him falling out if we got inverted. This was in the form of a cable from the floor, which was hooked on to a ring on the harness that he wore and which passed between his legs. It was very dangerous to stand up with your knees straight as your legs were locked beyond the straight position and if the aircraft imposed a high rate of 'G' your knees would be broken. The length of the cable was adjusted to a length so that the gunner could not quite stand up straight. As a result, if any 'G' was imposed, the gunner's knees bent and his legs were undamaged. This was extremely uncomfortable, but fortunately Hectors did not have a very long endurance and the gunner did not have to put up with the discomfort for long.

Return Flights in War and Peace

I was allotted to the north side of the town. It was a beautiful day, with no cloud and little wind, and we set off across the channel with some trepidation, not knowing what to expect, flying at 1,500 feet.

As we neared the coast all seemed quiet, though columns of smoke were rising in places. However, there seemed to be no enemy opposition. We started to fly around looking for targets, but could not see any. So we dropped one of our bombs. Then we dived down and fired our gun. After about ten minutes larking about and trying to make ourselves as conspicuous as possible and using up all our ammunition, with no stoppages fortunately, and thinking that by now the Lysanders had carried out their mission, I decided to head for home, despite not seeing any activity. I think that the Germans who had fired all the flak the previous day had moved on up the coast towards Dunkirk. We arrived safely back in Hawkinge with two others but one Hector crash-landed, badly damaged, on the cliffs of Dover and the pilot Pilot Officer Watkyn was killed. We had a bullet hole in our upper port wing, so somebody must have seen us. So, back to Odiham.

Two days later, the 29th, we went down to Hawkinge again, when the BEF was in an even smaller ring around Dunkirk. However, there was no task for us, and we were sent home unused.

As we all know, the BEF did get away from Dunkirk, so it could be said that the Hawker Hart/Hector played an important part in enabling Britain to carry on the war to ultimate victory. These were the only occasions on which such obsolete aircraft were used in Europe in the Second World War.

There was a very good feeling in the squadron when we received a commendation from the Air Officer Commanding the Group, and afterwards it was announced that two DFCs had been awarded to the Squadron. One was awarded to squadron Leader Anderson and the other one to Pilot Officer Al Edy. After all, they had both gone twice.

The citation for Edy's DFC was as follows;

> On 25 May 1940 Pilot Officer Edy was a member of a formation of aircraft detailed to carry out a dive bombing attack on a Heavy Battery near Calais. He pressed home his attack in the face of severe anti aircraft fire with the utmost courage. His bombs were observed to fall inside the target area and it was later reported that the battery had been moved. On 27 May 1940 this officer took part in low flying bombing and supply dropping sorties over the Calais garrison area and although his single front gun failed the raid was carried out at a very low altitude. By the skilful manipulation of his aircraft Pilot Officer Edy not only evaded the enemy anti-aircraft but also enabled his air gunner to put two machine gun posts out of action. He remained over the target, drawing the enemy fire to himself until the supply dropping aircraft no longer needed support. Pilot Officer Edy has shown a complete disregard of personal danger and has set a fine example by his keenness and magnificent spirit.

Shortly afterwards, we were told that our Hectors were going to be taken away and we would be equipped entirely with Lysanders. On 21 June I made my last flight in a Hector K 8111. In my youthful exuberance I had always wanted to dive a Hector to 250 miles an hour, but had always had to abandon the attempt because of over revving the engine. With our fixed pitch props we had the same problem as the early Spitfires and Hurricanes. As you dived faster, the revs went up so that you had to throttle back to keep the revs down. This, of course, stopped you going faster so your object was prevented. But, as these planes were going to be scrapped when I landed, I decided that I would have one last try. I went up to 12,000 feet, went into a dive and kept the throttle open. We were just approaching my target when there was an almighty crack and most of the fabric disappeared from the top of the top wing. The Hector wings, like all early aircraft, were covered in fabric over a framework of wooden ribs, all shrunk tight by applications of a liquid called dope. I hastily throttled back and pulled out of the dive. She was still flying normally so we landed without trouble, though there were a few odd looks from the ground crew.

One day, a group of us were standing on the tarmac at Odiham, watching a Lysander of another squadron approaching to land. Suddenly, for an inexplicable reason it put its nose down and dived into the ground where it exploded. We jumped into our cars and drove to the scene of the crash in a field about a mile away. When we got there, there was nothing we could do but play some fire extinguishers on the wreckage. After a few minutes I realized to my shock that what I was playing my own extinguisher on was the body of one of the crew. The smell was awful, just like roast lamb, and I had difficulty eating my lunch when we got back to the mess.

Chapter 7
Home Defence

After Dunkirk, all Army Co-op squadrons were back in England and with the new fear of invasion we were given the task of patrolling the coast at dawn and dusk in order to give early warning. Each squadron was given its own two areas. No. 613 Squadron was allotted the stretch of coast from Filey Point in Yorkshire to the Humber and from the Humber to the Wash. This necessitated a move northwards and we flew up to a drome called Netherthorpe near Worksop. This was only a field where a farmer kept his plane in a shed, a Klemm Swallow. It was just enough for our Lysanders to operate out of. A plane from each flight was detailed each day to fly out to the coast to patrol the coast for two hours before dusk. At dusk they went back to Finningley near Doncaster as Netherthorpe was not big enough for night landings. After spending the night at Finningley, they took off thirty minutes before dawn so as to be on the coast at first light. As this was midsummer whoever was on didn't get a very long night's sleep. While on the coast the pilot had to send situation reports by W/T every twenty minutes. Needless to say, these were nil reports always as they never came. I often wondered how anyone expected us to see them suddenly appear at the coast when the Navy had not noticed them coming all the way across the North Sea.

These patrols continued without much difficulty; everyone managed to get back to Finningley without too much trouble.

The thing was not to stay on the coast too late so that it got too dark before you got to Finningley. There was only a red beacon flashing in the blackout to tell where you were, but when they heard you they switched on the flare path.

Our flight commander was Flight Lieutenant Gus Weston, an officer called back from the reserve. He seemed very old to us at thirty-five and a bit past it. We wondered how he would get on when it became his turn. He put it off as long as he could but had to go in the end. Needless to say, he failed to find Finningley, and eventually had to land in the country. Fortunately, he did not hit anything when he hit the ground and the plane was only slightly damaged, while he was unhurt. So there was nobody patrolling one of the coastal areas in the morning, but as the invasion didn't materialize that didn't matter much.

Apart from these patrols the squadron did not have a lot to do, mainly co-operating with Army units while they carried out field days. When we landed near their headquarters we were taken to see the commanding general to tell him how easily we had been able to see his troops but they always retaliated by saying that we were so low that we would easily have been shot down.

When we moved to Netherthorpe, of course, there were no buildings there at all and we were operating just like an Army Co-operation squadron in the field. The ground handling facilities were so lacking that we did not even have a fuel bowser; all our fuel came in four-gallon disposable tins, which were stacked in large heaps. This made refuelling very hard for the ground staff. But one advantage for some with cars was that it was pretty easy for them to help themselves to a gallon or two, as petrol by now was severely rationed.

For an officers' mess we commandeered the local squire's mansion but this only provided the public rooms. There were no bedrooms and, believe it or not, I slept in a bell tent for a few weeks. I had obtained the standard type of camp kit when I was commissioned. This consisted of a camp bed with a wooden collapsible framework all rolled up in green canvas. I would like to say that I was quite comfortable but it was extremely cold at night even though it was mid-summer. I found out by experience that however much you piled on top it was not enough as the cold struck up from below. The secret was to put several layers of newspaper on the bottom, preferably *The Times*.

Things improved a bit later when we took over the porter's lodge at the end of the drive and Tiger and I moved in there, but with no furniture. We slept on the floor.

On 17 July John Sowrey and I borrowed the farmer's Swallow, which we had commandeered, and flew very slowly to Binbrook to see a couple of our Cranwell friends who were on Fairey Battles. We came in to land at 35 knots, after cruising at 60.

Netherthorpe was too small for anything but Lysanders and light planes to operate from. However, one day an Avro Anson landed, piloted by the wife of one of our gunners. She was in the ATA (Air Transport Auxiliary) and had called in to see him while on a delivery flight. We wondered if she would ever be able to get out of our small field. We pushed her plane right back until the rudder was touching the edge of the field. Then she set off at full bore. When she was nearly at the far edge of the field she was nowhere near take-off speed. The boundary was fortunately a low stone wall about four feet high. She hauled hard back on the stick and the Anson hopped over the wall and came down on the other side and ran on the grass for a couple of hundred yards before finally taking to the air.

We had one bad accident while we were there. As I returned from an exercise I saw a wrecked Lysander burning at the edge of the field. Apparently, a Lysander coming in to land had not noticed a lorry driving along the boundary and had caught it with his wheels, causing him to crash and explode. The gunner was OK but the pilot, Edmonds I believe, died in hospital that night.

One day in August, Bernard Brown rushed into the mess and said to me 'Have you heard the news? Most of us are going on Spitfires.' He said that twelve were to go and the flight commanders were in with the CO deciding who would go, so we rushed down to the adjutant's office where he confirmed the news. We waited outside, all praying that we would be selected, but when the news came out I was one of the four who stayed behind. This was a great disappointment but we just had to grin and bear it. Needless to say, Al Edy was one of those chosen to go. This was when the Battle of Britain was well under way and I was very sorry to hear that he had been killed in action a little later.

After a few weeks it was decided that Netherthorpe was not suitable any more so we moved to a slightly larger field at Firbeck. We settled in there quite well, though it was still a bit primitive, the officers' mess was a marquee. There was a lot of expectation that we were going to be invaded and there were lots of scares. On 8 September there was another one so I was sent off to Netherthorpe after breakfast with Sergeant Conacher in the back to await further instructions. Two planes went, the other flown by Pilot Officer Bennett. We got bombed up and had the tanks filled and then sat and waited to be sent off to repel the *Wehrmacht*. And waited. And waited. And waited. Absolutely nothing happened.

There were no catering facilities at Netherthorpe and I was beginning to get very hungry so I thought 'I'll nip over to the farmhouse over there and see if they can do anything for us.' So I went there and knocked on the door. When the lady came to the door I explained our predicament and she immediately became very sympathetic and said 'Poor things, come in and

Home Defence

I'll fix you up with some lunch.' We went in and she sat us down in the living room and produced a delicious lunch for us. The pudding was an apple sponge and custard, which was so superb that I have remembered it ever since, and every time that pudding has come on the menu I have bored my family rigid with my description of it.

Needless to say, it was another false alarm, and later in the day we were called back to Firbeck.

Chapter 8

Instructor Course at CFS

On 21 September I was called in to the CO's office and was told that I had been posted to the Central Flying School for a flying instructors' course. This was not very welcome news as I did not think it would be good for my career in wartime. But as it was an Air Ministry posting there was no objecting to it, so I said goodbye and left for Upavon on Salisbury Plain.

The CFI turned out to be Wing Commander Speedy Holmes who had been CFI at Cranwell after Wing Commander Boyle left at the beginning of the war. As a regular, I decided that, although I hated the posting, it was not the right thing to do to try and do badly and get thrown off the course, so I determined to do my best. The result was that when I left I got a very good assessment: 'will make a first class instructor.'

The art of instructing people to fly had been studied from the early days of the Royal Flying Corps when the Central Flying School was formed at Gosport. The name had been remembered in the Gosport tubes that were used for communication between the pupil and the instructor. This system comprised a tube about half an inch in diameter, which passed from cockpit to cockpit. One end had a mouthpiece that could be spoken into. The other end fitted into a tube that divided into two and led by pipes to the earpieces in the other pilot's flying helmet. This apparatus was duplicated. This enabled the two pilots to talk to each other perfectly plainly above the noise of the engine. This was very similar to the system on board ship that enabled somebody on the bridge to talk to someone in the engine room.

The different items of instruction had been analyzed and divided into a sequence of instructions divided into twenty-two parts, starting with No. 1, air experience, and progressing to No. 22, aerobatics, providing instruction in everything that was needed to become a qualified pilot. There was a small book that provided a note of what the instructor should say in order to instruct the pupil in the exercise that was being demonstrated. This was called the instructor's 'patter', and had to be learnt. The method of instruction was to give a demonstration of the lesson and then to allow the pupil to do it himself. The important part was that when giving the demonstration and giving the patter the synchronization was correct. For instance, when one was giving a demonstration of a take–off, the instructor should say 'The aircraft leaves the ground' at the same time as the aircraft did, in fact, leave the ground and was not flying at five hundred feet. This was quite a difficult thing to learn.

The other thing that instructors had to do was to teach their pupils to recover from any awkward situation in which they might find themselves. This was called limit flying, and was the reason that aerobatics were taught, No. 22 in the list. No. 7, taking off onto wind, and Nos 8 and 9, power and glide approach and landing respectively, were the necessities before going solo, particularly when converting on to a new type of aircraft, when little else was required.

Taking off and landing straight into the wind were vitally important in light aircraft where the flying took place on grass airfields where there were no runways. It was essential to view the windsock. If you were not directly into wind on landing you landed with drift, which could damage the undercarriage. But with the advent of larger and heavier aircraft, needing runways landing with a crosswind of some strength was almost always necessary, and the answer was to straighten up just before you touched down. Airfields were built with the longest runway constructed in line with the prevailing wind, usually due east and west. With two shorter runways on different directions for use where crosswinds were too strong, it was known, very occasionally, for pilots to misread the windsock and try to land downwind. In this case, of course, instead of the ground speed being the airspeed minus the wind speed, it was the airspeed plus the wind speed and the resulting ground speed was so high that it was impossible to get down. I have never heard of anybody managing to land downwind. They invariably managed to realize their mistake and land the right way with their tail between their legs, hoping that nobody had seen them.

There was one type of instruction that was not in the list and which was taught to single-engined pupils. This was formation flying and I did a lot of this later on Masters. This was essential for pupils who subsequently went on to fighters. But, strangely enough, it turned out that in Fighter Command close formation was not too good a thing as it took up far too much of one's attention to fly close, attention that was better employed in keeping a lookout for the enemy. The Germans had found this out in the Spanish Civil War. But it was not long before the RAF got the message and employed a much wider formation called the finger four, where fighters flew much wider apart in pairs and could watch each other's tails without any risk of collision.

This, of course, did not apply to larger aircraft. The American Flying Fortresses flew in formation as close as they could manage. But, in their case, the pilot had nothing else to do and could give all his attention to his flying while his many gunners kept a lookout.

Instructor Course at CFS

At CFS, the elementary instruction was done on Tutors, which I had flown at Cranwell, but we were also introduced to the latest very modern service trainer, the Miles Master. These were really up to date and equipped with Kestrel engines, which were from all the Hawker Harts and had been refurbished and fitted with superchargers to plus-8 boost. They also had retractable undercarriages and constant speed props so that after being trained on them pupils could go on Spitfires and Hurricanes without trouble. They were also fitted with the standard flying panel, which was becoming universal in all new RAF aircraft. The only trouble with them was that they were built of wood and not too strong so they were restricted to an airspeed of 285 miles per hour, which was quite enough to do any sensible aerobatics. Also, on the early ones the elevators were a little weak and inclined to fall off when overstressed, resulting in quite a few fatal accidents.

Fortunately, by the time I got on them this fault had been rectified. There was a story that at one of the flying schools, Montrose I believe, there had been yet another fatal accident one morning. One of the medical orderlies walked into the mess hall where the pupils were having lunch and announced, 'You chaps will have to be more careful, standing room only in the morgue now.'

Chapter 9

Instructor at Montrose

The course lasted a month, after which there was the choice between the two Master FTSs at Montrose in Scotland and Sealand in Shropshire. There was also the chance of going to Canada to take part in the Empire Training Scheme that was starting up. But I had the idea that if I went there I would never get back so I managed to avoid that, although as it turned out people were posted back to England after two years. Anyway, I was posted to Montrose on the Scottish coast between Aberdeen and Dundee. On arrival, I found out that the CFI was my ex-flight commander from Cranwell, now promoted to Squadron Leader Slater who I had always liked very much. The OC Flying was Wing Commander Macintyre, also an ex-Cranwell cadet, so I was lucky to have superior officers whom I liked and respected.

My flight commander was Flight Lieutenant Frankie Aikens. He was a bit of a character and had just finished a tour in Bomber Command in Whitleys and was renowned for being an expert on dive bombing in them. Six months later he was posted as chief flying instructor at Church Fenton, the newly formed Night Fighter OTU (Operational Training Unit) where his experience of night flying in Whitleys made him ideal for the job. At that time night flying could be extremely dangerous if you did not know what you were doing because of the blackout, which made it pitch black with no horizon when there was no moon, and there were quite a lot of fatal accidents. These included Richard Hillary, who was sent on night fighters by someone who thought it would be safer for him than going back on day fighters after the terrible experiences he had gone through on them. (Hillary had been shot down in 1940 while flying day fighters. He was very badly burned and treated by Dr McIndoe. He wrote *The Last Enemy*, which was about his experiences.) Sadly, Hillary later crashed and was killed. But at Montrose in summer night flying caused no problems because it was so far north that the sun hardly went below the horizon before it came up a couple of hours later.

The airfield was on the shore, separated from the sea by a line of sand dunes. A flight of Hurricanes from No. 111 Squadron were stationed there for protection against enemy hit and run attacks. Their dispersal was the other side of the drome from us and in the event of a raid warning they scrambled in a hurry regardless of anybody else, firing off a red Verey light as a warning. As their take-off run was usually at right angles to the landing run of all our Masters, we had to keep a good lookout and there were some hairy moments.

The camp was a First World War one and entirely made of timber. Our flight office at dispersal was an old aircraft crate but it sufficed. There was no room in the officers' mess for me so I was billeted in the best hotel in the town, which was quite satisfactory. A few days later I went down with flu and had to be confined to bed. A few days later I was lying in bed having my tea when I heard the sound of aero engines overhead and machine gun fire, followed a few seconds later by loud explosions. It turned out that a Heinkel had carried out a sudden raid, dropping a stick of bombs across the drome. One of them scored a direct hit on the officers' mess. The roof disappeared and the four sides fell flat. There were two people sitting in armchairs waiting for their tea and they found themselves reading their papers in the open air, completely unharmed. The bomb landed in the kitchen and scattered burning coals from the stove all over the wreckage and the whole lot went up in smoke. It turned out quite well for me because when I left Upavon I had left my gas mask and steel helmet behind and I was worrying about how I could replace them. Fortunately I 'remembered' that I had left them hanging on a hook in the hall of the now flattened mess, so I was able to replace them free of charge as destroyed by enemy action.

It turned out very well in another way. We now had no officers' mess so we were able to commandeer a large house on the outskirts of the town, which was much more comfortable.

Life as a flying instructor was reasonably pleasant. The pupils were very keen and discipline was no problem as they knew that if they did anything seriously wrong they would be turned off the course, though I only remember one pupil who never finished, and he failed because he just did not have the ability as a pilot. He had been a pupil at Shawbury when he was turned off, but he had a father with influence somewhere, a friend of the Secretary of State for Air I believe, who managed to get him a second chance so he was sent to us to see what we could do. The CFI sent for me and explained the situation and said that he was allotting him to me as my pupil to see what I could do with him. Unfortunately, it was no use; he seemed to have a very poor judgement of distance. On the first time he went solo at night he hit the ground a few hundred yards short of the runway, and he got very badly burned in the resulting crash. That was the end of his flying career. It was a great shame as he was incredibly keen to become a fighter pilot. It was some comfort to me that I was not instructing him on the night when he crashed.

Instructor at Montrose

Night flying at Montrose was pretty primitive. Being a grass drome, there were no electric flares on the flare path; we had to use gooseneck flares. These consisted of a watering can filled with paraffin and a wick reaching to the spout. This was set alight and provided a very good flare path. But it had several disadvantages. Firstly, it was very laborious setting out the flares, and secondly, if the wind changed it was a lot of work to change the runway. Lastly, it was very slow to extinguish in the event of an air raid. There was the old joke that night flying had to be cancelled one night because nobody had remembered to take any matches.

In May, a new course arrived that consisted mainly of Poles. They were very keen and had had varying amounts of training back home, but the Air Ministry decided to put them all through RAF training from the beginning. This upset some of them and one of them was heard to say to his instructor 'You think I know f*** nothing. But you are wrong. I know f*** all.' But one thing they had in common – they all hated Germans. One day a German bomber was shot down near Montrose and the one survivor, badly injured, was being treated in the sick quarters. All our Poles were waiting outside. Eventually, a man came out and announced that he had died. The Poles raised a cheer that raised the roof. We had a Polish instructor in each flight to help with the language problem, though their English was usually surprisingly good. The one in my flight was Sergeant Switon.

Another good story was when a few Polish officers were posted to a squadron and a party was given to welcome them. The station commander's wife attended and asked one of them, 'Are you married?' He replied 'Yes, but she is still in Poland.' 'What about children?' she asked. 'None', he replied, 'unfortunately my wife is inconceivable.' Another of the Poles standing with them said, 'My friend has made a mistake, he means she in impregnable.' A third one said, 'He is wrong too. What he should have said is she is unbearable.' The one in the other flight unfortunately was the cause of the most horrifying fatal accident I have ever seen, particularly as it caused the death of someone else.

The course in the other flight had finished their flying and were spending their last day tidying their paperwork, log books etc. The Pole picked randomly one of the pupils and said 'Come with me, I'll show you how to really fly one of these things.' They took off in a Master then started to give an aerobatic display. The Master was restricted to a speed of 285 miles per hour. I do not know what speed he got up to at the bottom of a dive but it was far too fast, and as a result of the strain put on the wings one of them snapped off like a carrot. He went vertically into the ground where the aircraft shattered into pieces. We inspected the site later and there wasn't a piece bigger than a handkerchief. I was flying in the circuit at the time and I shall never forget the sight of it as if went vertically down past us.

It was a regulation that pupils were not allowed to fly an aircraft until it had had an air test. If it was used for the first time in the day to give dual that was no problem, but if we wanted to send someone off solo we had to test it first, which consisted of a quick circuit and landing. One day on one of these tests, while on the downwind leg at 1,000 feet, the engine stopped. After a few seconds checking, I realized there was only one way to go – down. Fortunately, there was a convenient field nearby and we glided down and made a wheels-up landing, which was the correct thing to do. When I climbed out one of our lorries was passing so I got a quick lift back to base. I never did discover why the engine stopped.

After a time the supply of new Masters dried up as there were no more Kestrel engines to refurbish, and we became short of aircraft. There were a lot of Mark 1 Hurricanes in storage as they had been replaced in the squadrons by more up-to-date models. These were the planes that, when they first came out, were such a huge advance on the biplanes that they had flown before, the fighter boys had been swaggering about with their top buttons undone. They told everybody who would listen that only the very best pilots were allowed to fly them and they were not allowed to do aerobatics until they had done 100 hours in them.

Anyway, we went and collected a bunch of Hurricanes from the maintenance units where they were stored. In due course our pupils flew them with no trouble; people who had not even qualified for their wings, which were allotted at the end of their course. There was one snag that we quite liked. They could not be flown by the pupils each day until they had been tested, so I have piled up quite a few hours on Hurricanes, ten minutes at a time. A quick circuit is not very exciting but quite good fun.

But, something much better turned up. As all our pupils went on Spitfires when they left it was thought that it would be a good idea if some of us went down to the Spitfire OTU at Grangemouth to find out whether the pilots we were sending to them were satisfactory. On 15 June I went there for a week's attachment.

They seemed reasonably satisfied but the aerobatics of some were not too good. They had a Miles Master there on which the instructors were supposed to give the poorest pupils a little help. Unfortunately, they were averse to flying the Masters as they had heard of their reputation as being a little weak. Not having these fears, I volunteered to do a little of that flying for them. This earned me quite a few brownie points, so in response they were very generous in letting me fly their Spitfires and I got in well over ten hours on them while I was there, including a battle climb to 15,000 feet over Edinburgh.

Return Flights in War and Peace

I was able to assure the CFI on my return that all the unsatisfactory pilots had been trained at the other Master school.

Chapter 10

Instructor at CFS

On 28 July I was called into the CFI's office and informed that I had been posted to the CFS (Central Flying School). This was a great surprise to me as it was a great honour. Squadron Leader Slater congratulated me and I set off on the long journey to Upavon in my car. As the route passed close to Firbeck I called in to see them and on 30 July I borrowed a Lysander for a quick trip. The experience confirmed my opinion that I was well out of them. As a matter of fact, they were shortly re-equipped with Mustangs, but with the Allison engine, which had a very poor performance at altitude but was excellent at low heights where 613 Squadron would be operating, doing army reconnaissance. Later, they were re-equipped with Mosquitoes in which they did sterling work, including the famous bombing of the *Gestapo* building in the middle of the Hague at low level.

While I was at Montrose, I had gained the nickname Fingers – something to do with playing cards. I disliked this but I knew that the more I objected the more it would be used. So I just had to put up with it. When I was posted to Upavon I thought that I would be able to get free of it. Unfortunately, when I arrived and walked into the officers' mess, who should be sitting in the hall but Pete Prioleau who had been an instructor with me at Montrose.

'Fingers', he called out, 'what are you doing here?' So I was stuck with the name for a little longer.

On booking into headquarters I got a bit of a bollocking from the CFI, Wing Commander Holmes, but I explained that I had come by car and the long journey had taken a long time.

I was put in A Flight, which flew Masters. B and C Flights flew Oxfords. The Masters were the new type that were fitted with Twin Wasp radial engines. These gave a little more power but upset the balance a bit so they were not quite so nice to fly. They also had the fault of being a bit difficult to start if they were not primed correctly.

If overprimed with fuel they could backfire and a cloud of burning vapour enveloped the cockpit. There was a great inclination to get out and run, but the airman in attendance would shout 'Keep the button pressed!' It would start eventually and when it did it sucked all the flames up into the air intake and all was well. In A Flight we also gave instruction in the Tutors, which was a bit tedious.

There were several of the NCO instructors from Cranwell there, all now commissioned: Ginger Varley, Knocker West and Sam Booker. Pete Prioleau, another old friend from Montrose, was in A Flight with me. A bit of good news just after I arrived was that the new rule at CFS was that all instructors were flight lieutenants. This was great news, with an increase of pay that was very welcome, although it was a long time, not until the end of 1943, before I got any more promotion.

My posting to CFS also changed my life in another way. There were six WAAF officers stationed there. One of them was Section Officer Jean McMichael who was the cypher officer. We became friendly and later, when we were separated by postings, we kept in touch. To keep it short, we were married in May 1944 when I was in 625 Squadron and we had two fine sons, Michael and Philip.

Jean was a regular WAAF who had joined up before the war as a teleprinter operator. She was called up when the war

INSTRUCTOR AT CFS

started and her first posting was operating in a huge operations centre in northern England, where she worked several floors below ground level and she never saw daylight during working hours. Nothing but bright artificial lighting all the time. As a result, she became a little claustrophobic and hated working in artificial light for the rest of her life. In the event, her work was very satisfactory and she was recommended for a commission, and in 1942 her first posting as an assistant section officer was as cypher officer to Upavon where the CFS was based, and where we met. She was very proud of having served right through from before the war until the end and as I had also done the same we must have been one of the very few married couples who had twelve years' war service between us.

The flying at CFS was very different because the pupil was learning to be an instructor, so he sat in the instructor's seat, and I sat in the first pilot's seat, which was a lot more comfortable to fly in. The pupils, of course, were qualified pilots who had just finished tours of operations and were going to instruct at OTUs where they had to convert their pupils on to whatever service type of plane was there. Needless to say, they were a very happy bunch of people.

My brother David was a lieutenant in the Royal Welch Fusiliers and stationed near Salisbury, not far away. On 17 August 1941 he came to visit me. I took him up for a flight in a Master, which he enjoyed as I did not make him sick with lots of aerobatics, only a loop. When we landed he was amazed that I had been able to find my way back to the aerodrome as he had been completely lost because of the confusing sight of the patchwork of fields below. I explained that it was easy as you soon learned the lie of the country, but you had to beware of agricultural changes. I remember when I had not been at Cranwell very long and my instructor had pointed out a field below that was a very good landmark as the crop was mustard and the yellow-coloured field was very conspicuous. It was very useful until the day it disappeared because the farmer had harvested it.

In March 1942 my brother came for a visit again and while he was there he received a telegram to say that he had been posted out to India and must report back to base forthwith for immediate posting. 'What can I do?' David asked. 'How can I get back quickly?' I said I would fly him back to Warmwell, which is a drome near his unit, and with luck I would fly him back to see our parents on the way as they lived very near St Athans in South Wales. I went to see the CFI and explained the situation to him and he immediately authorized me to take David back via St Athans and Warmwell. That is what we did. When we parted from my mother she gave him half a dozen eggs, which were like gold in those days. When we got to the plane for the flight to Warmwell I told him to hand me the eggs, which were in a paper bag, and I would put them in his hat upside down on his suitcase, stored in the fuselage behind the rear seat. I climbed up and put them there. When we got to Warmwell, he climbed down and stood waiting for me to hand down his luggage. I knelt on the back seat then picked up his hat containing the bag of eggs and handed it down to him. Without thinking, he took the hat and put it on his head. I would like to be able to relate that the broken eggs ran down all over his head, but fortunately not. The paper bag did not break and only the eggs were a casualty.

I did not see David for several years until he came back from India. I have to say that I was a great deal luckier than him as during his absence I lived in comfort at various RAF stations, while after a time in the Punjab he had a particularly unpleasant time in the jungle in Burma, with torrential rain, mud, malaria, pests and misery of all kinds, to say nothing of the Japanese.

INSTRUCTOR AT CFS

Upavon had an extremely comfortable mess, which was brick built. It even had a nine-hole golf course with the first tee on the opposite side of the road to the front door of the mess. So I took up golf.

Unfortunately, Pete Prioleau became involved in an accident with me that turned out very badly for him. He and I flew to Cranfield to take two WAAF officers for a visit. After dropping them off we taxied off around the perimeter track. There was a runway control officer at the end of the runway in a caravan; one had to get a green light from him before entering the runway. I got a red light from him so I waited on the perimeter track, while I watched the plane approaching to land. It was a Douglas Havoc, a night fighter version of the Boston, and the nose was covered with an array of radar aerials. Unfortunately, Pete also became very interested in watching the Havoc, so much so that he forgot about me. The first I knew was when my plane started to shake and judder. His prop was chewing up the back of the plane like a bacon slicer. Fortunately, he came to his senses before it came to me and switched off. But both planes were a write-off. We had to get a lift back to Upavon in a Blenheim.

It is an understanding in the RAF that flying is a dangerous game, and some accidents can be viewed with a little sympathy. But there is one type of accident for which there is no excuse – even for a pupil pilot. That is a taxiing accident. For a qualified pilot it is even worse. For a flying instructor even worse still, but for an instructor at the CFS it didn't bear thinking about. Pete's interview with the CFI was not a happy one and he was posted away shortly afterwards. He went into Bomber Command flying Stirlings and was shot down and killed. It was a great tragedy as he was one of my best friends. Fortunately, as the innocent party I was in the clear.

Shortly afterwards, who should appear in the mess but Squadron Leader Slater, the CFI from Montrose. He was passing through on his way to a Spitfire OTU, and had a permanent grin from ear to ear. He was one of the happiest officers in the RAF. Unfortunately, a few months later I saw his name in the casualty lists as killed in action – another sad loss.

Another occasional visitor to the mess was an ex-instructor, Wing Commander Salter, a charming and very popular officer. He was stationed at Boscombe Down where he was carrying out trials in the Lancaster, the new heavy bomber that was beginning to appear. He was carrying out a diving speed trial when a panel came loose in the wing and he was unable to pull out, with fatal results. So for me it was not a very happy time.

For some time I had been thinking that I ought to be able to fly twins, and when I mentioned this to my friend Flight Lieutenant Olley, he suggested that he would give me the necessary instruction in his spare time. So on 9 August 1941 he took me up in an Oxford and I went solo on them. There was a twin-engined Dominie twelve-seater Transport plane that was used to take people to New Zealand Farm for night flying, and I cadged as many flights as possible in it. Also, when possible I got in some flying in an Oxford. However, it was still a bit of a surprise when in February 1942 the CFI sent for me and told me he was putting me in B Flight. 'But they are on Oxfords,' I said. 'I know', he said, 'but you'll manage.'

As the CFI had said, I managed without any trouble; after all, my pupils were all experienced multi-engined pilots. One I remember was Flight Lieutenant Mahaddie who had just finished a tour on Whitleys and was instructing at Lossiemouth. He later did another tour on Stirlings and became a big cheese in the Pathfinder Force as the officer in charge of recruiting suitable crews for them. He finished up as a group captain and, post war, had quite a career as an adviser for films about the RAF. At the time he was on the

INSTRUCTOR AT CFS

staff at Abingdon, which was a Whitley OTU, and one day he took me over there and gave me a flight in an early version of the Whitley with radial engines. I could not believe how heavy the controls were and wondered how anybody could manage them for very long.

In May 1942 came the news of the first thousand bomber raid on Cologne. I remember this was a great stimulus in morale to me and the whole nation. We felt that we were at last doing something to win the war. I wondered again how much longer I would be a flying instructor.

Shortly afterwards, there was a reorganization of CFS. A new unit called the Empire Central Flying School (ECFS) was to be formed at Hullavington and Upavon was to become No. 7 Flying Instructors' School (FIS). A lot of our people went to it but not me. The instruction at ECFS was to be less on flying and more on the theoretical side and I am sure that I was a little young for the job, being only twenty-three.

In August 1942 I was posted to No. 3 FIS at Castle Combe. It was a grass drome with a tarmac perimeter track, which was bought from the Air Ministry after the war and used for motor racing.

Chapter 11

Bomber Command at Hixon OTU

On 16 February 1943 I was posted to No. 30 OTU at Hixon, near Stafford, in Bomber Command, where they flew Wellingtons. This, for me, was a welcome change after two and a half years as a flying instructor, although not without a little trepidation. I knew that there were considerable risks involved, but I had enough confidence in myself to think that I would be OK. Of course, as I was now flying twins, I had lost my chance to go on to Spitfires, but there was nothing I could do about it, so I determined to make the most of it.

One advantage of this posting was that I had gone to a new unit of the RAF where nobody knew me and I was finally able to say goodbye to my nickname, and for the rest of my career anybody who wanted to called me Roly.

The instruction at Hixon was carried out in courses, when a number of newly qualified pilots were put together in an empty hangar with a similar number of navigators, wireless operators, bomb aimers and air gunners and told to sort themselves into crews who would from then onwards fly together. I had arrived as a one-off, so this situation might have created a problem. But I was very lucky that one pilot had broken a leg playing rugby and was likely to be off flying for some time, so I was allotted his crew. The navigator was Sergeant Derrick Parry, a slim, fair-haired chap, always immaculately dressed. I remember him telling me that he was convinced that appearance was extremely important. His mother had once told him, 'Remember that there's always an eye on you.' I was very confident in him as a navigator; his work was always as immaculate as his appearance. The bomb aimer, Sergeant Ken Kennedy, was an Irishman who had started his career preparing to be a priest, although one would never have thought so. The wireless operator (W/Op) was Eddie Stainer and the rear gunner was Sergeant Pete (Joe) Lyons. Pete was a Londoner and very much a streetwise man of the world. He was very keen to be as good as he possibly could at his job, as indeed were they all.

They were a grand bunch and had done quite a bit of flying together as a crew. I took to them straight away and I think they took to me. I think we were all pleased at what we had got. They called me Skipper and I called them by their Christian names. Because I was a pilot I had to do the full course, which meant that they had to do it all again, which I think was an advantage. You cannot do too much training. I never had a cross word with any of them, except once near the end of our course, due to a misunderstanding.

We had done everything that we had to do, except that Pete had not finished the gunnery exercises that were necessary. This consisted of camera gun exercises on a drogue towed by a Miles Martinet. Unfortunately, the only pilot of the Martinet was sick and so there was a hold up in the gunnery training. Now it happened that a Martinet was only a Miles Master fitted up as a target tower, the cockpit was exactly the same. So I explained to the flight commander that I wanted to get my gunner to finish his training and asked if I could fly the necessary exercise. He immediately agreed and on 17 April 1943 I did a ninety-minute flight in the Martinet and my crew were finished. Unfortunately, when Pete saw me flying the Martinet he came to a hasty conclusion and accused me of chickening out of the crew for a nice safe job. However, when I explained to him that I had only flown the Martinet in order to enable him to finish his course and would not be flying it any more, it was all cleared up. All was sweetness and light again.

The flying was done in Wellingtons. To my surprise, these were the very latest type and almost new. They even had the latest type of electrically operated constant speed props.

I imagined that this was because the squadrons were now being supplied with heavies and Wellingtons were now relegated to training. By now I had done over 1,600 hours flying and I had no trouble going solo after three and a half hours' dual.

The ground lectures were a real eye-opener. In Training Command we had not been privy to operational information but now we were in Bomber Command there was an operations room where a lot of secret information was available. We also had lectures on subjects such as how to behave if one was taken prisoner and how to get in touch with the escape organizations (do nothing and wait for them to get in touch with you).

Another lecture we had was from an Army officer in the artillery who told us about flak, which was the German name for anti-aircraft. He told us that there were two sorts, light and heavy. The light was fired in groups of ten or so tracer shells. It was deadly but only fired up to about 3,000 feet. The heavy flak fired shells that were not visible until they burst with a puff of smoke in daylight or a flash at night. They were very accurate up to about 18,000 feet. But this fell off very rapidly above this height, so as we were in Lancasters we would be flying at 20,000 and should not get too much trouble from it. This would later turn out to be nonsense.

Yet another lecture that we had at Hixon was about the other danger that we were to face, the German night fighters. The Germans had developed a system called the Kammhuber Line, named after General Kammhuber. The line stretched from Denmark down to France, so that it was not possible to fly to Germany without passing through it. The line was divided up into boxes. Each box had a radar set, which was able to locate any aircraft that penetrated its airspace. Each box also had a night fighter, also equipped with air-to-air radar. When a hostile aircraft came past, the night fighter was directed by the ground control to the vicinity of the target and was then able to home on to it by using its own radar. The fighter would approach the target from behind and slightly below. This gave the fighter a great advantage as he could see the bomber fairly well against the starry sky, whereas the fighter was much more difficult to see against the dark ground. The fighter could also see the bomber's exhausts from behind whereas its own were invisible from the front.

This sounded a bit disturbing, but we did have a tactical countermeasure. This consisted of saturation of the defences. If a single aircraft tried to penetrate the line by itself it could be easily dealt with, but if we all bunched together to rush the defences there were only so many that the fighters could deal with. Accurate navigation was therefore very important to make sure that we all went through the same box, and did not stray into the next box all by ourselves, where we could be easily picked off. Timing was also important to make the concentration of the bomber stream as good as possible.

We also discovered how our bombers were able to find and bomb their targets in darkness. There had been an inquiry into the accuracy of the RAF's bombing and it had been discovered that it had been extremely inaccurate with only a very few bombs dropped within five miles of the target. An elite force of the best crews and navigators was formed, the Pathfinders, with Air Vice Marshal DCT Bennett in command. He was an RAF pilot who, when he retired, became an extremely successful pilot with Imperial Airways and a renowned navigation expert who had pioneered the Atlantic

Bridge for ferrying bombers from America to England. He set up a system in which several Pathfinders would drop lines of flares across the target, and then markers would identify the target by the light of the flares and drop Target Indicators (TIs) for the main force to bomb. The crews of the main force did not have to locate the target; they only had to be approximately in the right place at the right time and bomb the TIs when they appeared. If the TIs were in the wrong place it was not their responsibility. This required extremely accurate navigation and timing on the part of the Pathfinders, but they had the benefit of the new radar aid called H2S, which was carried in the aircraft and which would indicate to the operator the location of built-up areas and most accurately water, such as coastlines, lakes and large rivers. This was a very difficult system to operate but turned out to improve the bombing considerably.

There was another system called Oboe, which was operated by Mosquitoes. It worked with a system similar to a beam but relied on radar and was reputed to be accurate to within a hundred yards. The disadvantage of Oboe was that as it was radar operated it would only work within line of direct sight. The Mosquitoes therefore had to fly very high for the system to work, so they flew at a maximum altitude of 30,000 feet. This would be OK for targets in the Ruhr but for targets deeper in Germany, the other less accurate system had to be employed.

Radar was much more precise than radio and could measure distances very accurately. The system had two stations to operate it. All the first station had to do was to discover the exact distance to the target and then they could put a virtual circle through it that the receiver in the aircraft could read, so they could fly on a path that passed exactly over the target. The second station sent radar pulses to the aircraft, which had a transponder that sent a signal back to the station that was much stronger than a reflecting signal would have been. The second station was therefore able to very accurately monitor the progress of the aircraft towards the target and at the precise moment required to hit the target sent a Morse code signal for the navigator to release the TI.

The foundation of the Pathfinders was good news for us as it removed the responsibility of finding the target and circling about over the target area trying to locate the aiming point.

Another development that had taken place was that photographs were taken of where the bombs were dropped. As it was dark, the photographs were taken by a photo flash while the camera lens was open, in exactly the same way that I had taken my photographs at Cranwell. The camera lens was opened when the bombs were dropped and the photo flash fell out of its chute. The flare went off half a minute later when the plane was over the point where the bombs should have landed. They carried on with you below as they fell. As the camera lens was open any fires on the ground would show on the film as streaks, which spoiled the photograph, particularly for planes later in the attack. But it did put a stop to people claiming to have bombed the target when they had dropped them out in the country! The disadvantage for the pilot was that he had to stay straight and level for half a minute after 'bombs gone', when the inclination was to start taking evasion action.

It was then that I realized that our bombing was directed at whole towns and not at individual targets, but this did not worry me. I had suspected it for some time but thought it was justifiable retaliation for what the Germans had been doing to us.

It was at Hixon that I came across the new type of flare path that had been adopted by Bomber Command, called Drem lights, after Drem near Edinburgh, where they had been invented. In Training Command night flying was still done with a flare path consisting of goosenecks. Upavon was a dreadful field, completely unusable at night, and we had to go to a subsidiary field called New Zealand Farm where the gooseneck flare path was set out with a Chance light, a type of flood light that was set beside the start of the flare path.

The new airfields that were being built had runways to accommodate the new types of aircraft, and were fitted with subterranean electrical supplies to the flare path that could be switched on and off from the control tower. There was a line of hooded flares on each side of the runway. These were exactly like the catseyes that are on the roads today, so that they can only be seen from the side, but instead of reflectors they had bulbs inside. The result was the flare path could not be seen from above and therefore could not be bombed, and you could not see the flare path until you were on the final approach. To lead you on to the flare path there was a system of white lights called Drem lights, which were situated on top of poles about fifteen feet long and clearly visible all around. The drome from the air looked like a circle of lights about three miles across. Lincolnshire was covered with them. You could identify your own by what were called the Sandra lights, which consisted of one or more searchlights shining from different positions. The Sandra light at Wickenby was a single searchlight in the north-east of the ring of Drem lights, shining up at an angle of forty degrees. When you reached your base you flew a left-hand circuit around the outside of the Drem lights at 1,000 feet until you came to the lead-in lights, which led down to the funnel lights. You had by then lost height to 500 feet and the runway lights became visible. Landing was easy with the runway illuminated by a row of white lights at each side of the runway. When you reached the end of the runway you turned off on to the perimeter track, which was marked on both sides by pale blue glim lights, and proceeded to your dispersal. The lights were all controlled from the control tower, who would turn on the required lead-in lights and funnels for whichever runway was in use.

Of course, all the aircraft had R/T so that the flying control was able to control the movement of all the planes in the circuit by radio. This was a million miles away from Training Command where no aircraft had radio used for intercom on board. There, we only had the Gosport tubes, which of course were quite adequate for the purpose.

We were informed a few weeks after we started at Hixon that we would be going on Lancasters when we left. What a marvellous surprise that was, much better than I could have expected.

It was at Hixon that I first came across radar. This was in the form of Gee, a navigational aid that, by giving the positions where curves on charts crossed, would give you a position within a few yards. This was sensational, but after a time was only of use over England and the North Sea because the Germans found out how to jamb the signals once over enemy territory.

This prevented us from obtaining accurate fixes over Germany, but fixes were still available over the North Sea. Navigating is done by taking two fixes some distance apart and using the data by calculating the strength of the wind so that the next course can be calculated. These fixes are obtained when they are available and not necessarily when they are wanted and so the time between the fixes varies and the calculations are laborious and time consuming. But Gee enabled you to get a fix at any moment you wanted, down to the second. So the practice while crossing the North Sea was to take fixes at exactly six minutes apart, a period of a tenth of an hour. The calculations were therefore a lot simpler and quicker as a lot of the calculations were simply solved by multiplying by ten.

The course consisted of fifty hours' day and forty hours' night flying, which included several cross-country flights, plus practice bombing on the bombing range. Ken seemed to be quite an adequate bomb aimer and I was delighted to find that Derrick was an excellent navigator. Being a flight sergeant, he had done more than his initial training and was very experienced. As it was spring we were lucky in having good weather for our cross-countries. There were a lot of crashes at OTUs in winter with crews getting lost in bad weather and finishing up in the Welsh hills.

Near the end of the course we were given a mid-upper gunner, Sergeant Robinson, known as Robbie obviously! He was the most cheerful person I had ever come across, and had been an armourer before volunteering for aircrew. He was a real asset to the crew, though he had no turret until we got to the heavies.

The final flight at Hixon was a Bullseye, which was a dummy raid on a British town. This we carried out satisfactorily, though we were intercepted by a Mosquito night fighter.

This brought to an end our course on 20 April 1943 and we were sent off on a week's leave before reporting to 1656 Heavy Conversion Unit it Lindholme near Doncaster where we would convert on to heavies. We would also get a flight engineer to complete the crew.

I went on leave to where my parents lived near Cardiff, and after a few days I went down with influenza. My mother wanted to send for a doctor but I said airily 'Don't do that, send to the hospital at St Athans. They'll send someone out.' But I had miscalculated. An RAF ambulance arrived outside and two airmen with a stretcher came in and carried me away to hospital. I recovered after a few days but the doctor did not seem to want to let me go. Each day on his round, although I felt fully fit, he said 'We'd better keep you a bit longer to make sure.' I was very bored so I decided to go for a walk around the aerodrome, and to my delight I found that there was a Lancaster parked there that was used by the flight engineers' school that was situated there.

I walked up to the rear door and looked inside. I could hear someone moving about inside so I called 'Can I come in?' A voice replied 'Yes', so I climbed in and went up to the cockpit where I found a flight sergeant flight engineer. He said he had done a tour in Coastal Command on Catalinas and was now doing the course here and would be going to Lindholme on Lancasters in a few days. I said 'So am I' and as we liked the look of each other we agreed that if we met there we would crew up. This turned out for me to be one of the best things I ever did as he was a real treasure. He was very capable and experienced, and as steady as a rock.

I was allowed out at last and arrived at Lindholme on 1 May 1943, a bit worried that my crew had been given to somebody else. But, fortunately, they were still waiting for me and told me that a batch of new flight engineers was arriving. They would be on the tarmac at the flight office the next morning at nine o'clock and we would be allowed to choose one of them. I told them that I might already have one organized but did not elaborate. Sure enough, the next morning when the two groups were introduced to each other, the man I wanted was there. We recognized each other straight away and crewed up. His name was Charlie Edwards and his arrival completed my crew.

Nearly all crews consisted of aircrew who had just finished their training, but with my own experience, an experienced navigator, engineer and mid-upper gunner, I thought we had a better chance than most of getting through.

Lindholme was the conversion unit for No. 1 Group, with headquarters at Bawtry and commanding a group of squadrons at bases in North Lincolnshire.

All of their squadrons were equipped with Lancasters except for one Polish squadron, which still flew Wellingtons. Because the Lancaster was a much better plane than the Halifax, the Halifaxes were used for some of the training to convert us to four-engined aircraft.

I did my first flight in a Halifax on 21 May 1943 and after four and a half hours' dual went solo on 27 May. The Halifax was very different to anything I had flown before; the approach speed was very high but I soon got used to it. We only did circuits and landings in Halifaxes and while we did this I only carried the flight engineer and the wireless operator as we did not need the others.

After fifteen hours on the Halifaxes we transferred to the Lancaster flight and on 8 June I did my first dual with Flight Lieutenant Bob Noden. As the drome at Lindholme was very crowded we flew to Elsham Wolds, a No. 1 Group drome where 101 Squadron was based and which had little traffic. I went solo after two and a half hours. What a delight to fly after the Halifaxes.

Another marvellous addition to the Lancaster was the Distant Reading compass known as the DR compass, also mistakenly referred to as the Dead Reckoning compass. The master unit was situated back in the fuselage where the magnetic interference was at a minimum. Then it had repeater dials at several places as well as for the pilot who had one on his instrument panel. The navigator and bomb aimer were therefore also able to see what course was being steered. It was also linked to the auto pilot so that it would keep the aircraft on the course that was set on the pilot's dial, instead of gradually precessing off course as the American one did, like all gyros. In addition, if a small alteration of course was set the compass would steer the aircraft on to the new course.

After five hours of circuits we did a seven-hour day cross-country then after a few night circuits we did a six-hour night cross-country. Both of these were out over the Outer Hebrides as training flights were not permitted over the North Sea. This completed our training at Lindholme and we were ready for posting to a squadron.

Unfortunately, disaster struck. Up until now, if any aircrew suffered from VD, and as a result was classed as sick and unable to fly, their crew had been able to wait until they were recovered and fit again. But this was happening to so many people that it was beginning to interfere with the training program so a new order was introduced that in future if this happened the person concerned would lose his crew and a new person would be put in instead.

On 11 June Pete, the rear gunner, asked to speak to me and told me that he had got into trouble with a girl in Doncaster, and as a result he was off flying and being taken off my crew. This was dreadful news and I went to see the gunnery leader to ask what replacements were available. He told me that there was nobody trained available. The only person spare at the moment was a Sergeant Short who had been bypassed in the training program, had done no training at Lindholme, had done no night flying and only about ten hours' flying altogether. But he was all that available and he was to be put in my crew. This was a dreadful shock, but the crew rallied together to give him as much gen as they could, and he flew with us on our last two cross-countries. But he was obviously pretty clueless.

When I went to Lindholme I had asked which was a good squadron to go to. I was told that it did not matter a lot where one went but to stay away from 12 Squadron where the losses were horrendous. I had discovered that Wing Commander MacIntyre, the chief instructor at Montrose, was now the CO of 300 Squadron at Grimsby so I borrowed an Oxford and flew over to see him. He was pleased to see me and readily agreed with my suggestion that I should come to him when the time came and said he would arrange it. He telephoned Group and fixed it on the spot. I went back and told my crew the good news and they were suitably pleased. However, when we finished the course and went to get our posting I was dismayed to find that we had been posted to 12 Squadron. Apparently, they had lost five aircraft the previous night and their need for replacements overrode the arrangement I had made.

Chapter 12

First Tour in 12 Squadron

No. 12 Squadron was based at Wickenby, ten miles north-east of Lincoln. We went there on 20 June 1943 with three other crews.

It was a newly built camp, with Nissen huts of different sizes, even the officers' mess. But as it was mid-summer it was quite comfortable. As an officer I got half a Nissen hut to myself and the crew had a Nissen hut with eight beds to themselves with an airman, an Irish ACH called Paddy, to keep the place tidy and attend to their comfort.

We reported to the CO, Wing Commander Woods, a magnificent officer who on every trip of his tour took a new crew on their first trip. When he finished he was awarded a very much deserved DSO.

I was allotted to B Flight, together with Pilot Officers Lighton and Wally Snell. The flight commander was Squadron Leader Heyworth, DFC. He was on his second tour and thus would do only twenty trips, as opposed to thirty trips for a first tour, which is what we faced.

On 14 April there had been a low-level daylight raid by a squadron in 5 Group on the MAN U-boat engine factories in Augsburg. A lot of aircraft were shot down and the leader had been awarded a Victoria Cross. The citation was as follows:

> The KING has been graciously pleased to confer the VICTORIA CROSS on the under mentioned officer in recognition of most conspicuous bravery:-

Return Flights - In War and Peace

Acting Squadron Leader John Dering Nettleton (41452), No. 44 (Rhodesia) Squadron.

Squadron Leader Nettleton was the leader of one of two formations of six Lancaster heavy bombers detailed to deliver a low-level attack in daylight on the diesel engine factory at Augsburg in Southern Germany on April 17th, 1942. The enterprise was daring, the target of high military importance. To reach it and get back, some 1,000 miles had to be flown over hostile territory.

Soon after crossing into enemy territory his formation was engaged by 25 to 30 fighters. A running fight ensued. His rear guns went out of action. One by one the aircraft of his formation were shot down until in the end only his and one other remained. The fighters were shaken off but the target was still far distant. There was formidable resistance to be faced.

With great spirit and almost defenceless, he held his two remaining aircraft on their perilous course and after a long and arduous flight, mostly at only 50 feet above the ground, he brought them to Augsburg. Here anti-aircraft fire of great intensity and accuracy was encountered. The two aircraft came low over the roof tops. Though fired at from point blank range, they stayed the course to drop their bombs true on the target. The second aircraft, hit by flak, burst into flames and crash-landed. The leading aircraft, though riddled with holes, flew safely back to base, the only one of the six to return.

Squadron Leader Nettleton, who has successfully undertaken many other hazardous operations, displayed unflinching determination as well as leadership and valour of the highest order.

Squadron Leader Heyworth had a bee in his bonnet that we should do a raid of the same kind, and he had persuaded the CO to let us do daylight formation practices so that we could do the same thing. We did a couple of these practices but fortunately Group did not take the hint and nothing came of it, much to my relief as I did not relish going off on a suicide mission, particularly if someone else, Squadron Leader Heyworth, would have got the VC.

I was surprised to find that there were very few people on the squadron sporting medal ribbons. This was because most of the people in the squadron were early in their tours and had not had much chance to win them. Most were awarded at the end of a tour. The majority were worn by people on their second tour, like Squadron Leader Heyworth.

After the recent losses, morale was not exactly good. I had a drink in the sergeants' mess with the crew that evening and we all managed to convince ourselves that we would be OK.

Strangely enough, I don't know why, but during my time in B Flight we only lost one crew. We all finished our tours in my group, including Sergeant Murray Brown, an Australian who arrived just after us. But it was a different story in the other two flights; they were incurring losses one after the other.

We were given a week's leave every six weeks. What happened was that your name was put on the bottom of the list of pilots in the flight. When you got to the top of the list you went on leave, and when you came back you went to the bottom of the list. This had a disadvantage in B Flight (with fewer losses) as it was a long time until your next leave came due, unlike the other flights. One chap went on leave and when he came back he got up the list and went on leave again a fortnight later!

As we were a night bomber squadron, our working hours were designed to suit. When we returned from an operation it was usually in the early hours of the morning by the time we got to bed. The normal time for morning parade was therefore 11.30 am. Very gentlemanly – so if we were not flying we usually stayed up late.

When we turned up in the morning, the pilots congregated in the flight office. The other categories of aircrew went to their own offices. Then we just sat around until the decision came down from Group about whether we were operating that night. If ops were on, the flight commander decided who would fly that night and which plane they would fly. They would carry out a short test flight before the ground crews would bomb up and fuel the aircraft. A large fuel load and small bomb load indicated a long trip, whereas a small fuel load and maximum bomb load meant a short one, though the actual target was a secret until briefing. The time of briefing was worked back from the time of zero hour and the length of the trip.

If ops were not on, a small training programme would be decided on: test flights, bombing practice on the range on the Wash, fighter affiliation etc. Also, new crews would have to do a long cross-country.

But there was one advantage that we had in a bomber squadron as opposed to a fighter squadron. Once the decision had been made that we were not operating that night the squadron was stood down until the next day, and if we were not on the training programme we were free to go and do as we pleased. A trip in to Lincoln was a favourite, except that when you got there the pavements were crowded with men in RAF uniform.

This was the reason for the fiasco of the passage of the battleships *Scharnhorst* and *Gneisnau* from Brest, where they had been for a long time, back to Germany via the English Channel and the straits of Dover. Much was made in the press because Bomber Command had not been able to mount much of an attack against them. But it takes hours to bomb up and refuel a bomber squadron and it cannot be done until the

First Tour in 12 Squadron

target is known. Furthermore, armour-piercing bombs are needed against warships and these are not usually stocked on heavy bomber stations. In any case, they need to be dropped from high altitude so that they can build up enough velocity to penetrate armour. This was not possible as the weather was very bad with poor visibility, heavy rain and a cloud base at 1,000 feet. It was a task for torpedo bombers, but only a few were available and they were slaughtered when they made what was a suicide mission. The leader was awarded the Victoria Cross for his gallant failure in face of overwhelming opposition. Since the warships were not noticed until they were well up into the Channel it is not surprising that Bomber Command were not able to do very much.

In a fighter squadron it is very much different. It is not really widely appreciated that bombers are an offensive weapon and can operate against the enemy at any time that they think is suitable. But fighters are a defensive weapon and can only operate when the enemy comes to them. As a result, they have to be ready to go into action at any time at a moment's notice. This results in fighter pilots having to hang around for long periods at readiness with their aircraft fully fuelled and armed so that they can jump aboard and leave the ground in under two minutes. While I had been instructing at Montrose, I had been attached to a fighter squadron near Edinburgh for a week for experience. It was the most boring week I have ever experienced. The enemy never came and all we did for the whole week was wait in the crew room with nothing to do. We were never completely released as when the other flights were on readiness we were kept on thirty minutes' standby to take their place if they were scrambled.

On 22 June we did our first flight in the squadron, fighter affiliation for forty minutes. Then on the next day we did an air test and at night a four and a half-hour night cross-country.

Return Flights in War and Peace

After the fighter affiliation flight I put up a bit of a black by landing at the wrong drome, Faldingworth, a few miles away. It was also ten miles north-east of Lincoln and looked very like Wickenby, so there was some excuse as this was my first flight from base. But it was just carelessness. Anyway, I saw what had happened as soon as we touched down. I took off again before anybody noticed.

Wally Snell had an amazing experience on his cross-country. The route was from Wickenby to Land's End, then back up to the Outer Hebrides and back to base. When he landed he was greeted with lots of congratulations. 'What for?' Wally asked. 'For the German fighter you shot down.' 'What fighter?' he asked. Apparently, as he was flying at 20,000 feet in the vicinity of Cornwall, a Messerschmitt 109 flying at about 30,000 feet had dived down vertically to attack him and had carried on vertically until it hit the ground. The Observer Corps had seen this and assumed that his gunners had shot it down. This sounds a bit of a tall story but I can swear that is how it was told to me.

Low flying below 3,000 feet was strictly prohibited, although very enjoyable, but there was no restriction over the sea. So, on a test flight we used to take a trip from Mablethorpe to Skegness at low level, a few hundred yards out from the shore. I have happy memories of looking up at the people leaning over at the end of Skegness pier looking down at us.

One day there was no wind and the sea was like a sheet of glass, so we came right down. Charlie stood with his head in the blister where he could see straight down. We inched down until the tips of the props started to make eddies on the surface of the water and Charlie told me to hold it. Then we held it, and had a fantastic sensation of speed.

After our night cross-country on 23 July we were fully operational. So when ops were on it was our turn to go.

First Tour in 12 Squadron

There were two systems by which pilots did their first trip. One method was that the pilot went as a passenger with an experienced crew. In the other way, an experienced pilot took your crew with you as second pilot. In my case, I went as a passenger with Flight Sergeant Wells on his twenty-fourth trip.

The fuel load was 1,400 gallons so it was going to be a short trip. Briefing was at 18.00 hours, and I sat with Wells and his crew. The back of the room was covered by a large map, but this was covered by a curtain. When the briefing started the curtain was drawn back and we saw that the target was Gelsenkirchen, an oil refinery town in the Ruhr. The route to and back from the target was marked with red tape.

There was a board giving details of the aircraft going and the attack was divided into five-minute waves with different types of aircraft in each group. There were two Lancaster waves, two Halifax waves and one Stirling wave, with about 100 planes in each wave. The total number of aircraft was about six hundred. One of the Lancaster groups was the first group, the other one the last. As an experienced pilot Wells was in the first wave. The CO started the proceedings by pointing out the target then handed over to the intelligence officer who gave all the details of the attack. Zero hour was 23.00 hours.

The TIs would be red ground markers, dropped by Pathfinder Mosquitoes using Oboe. In case of cloud, red sky markers would be dropped. Green TIs as backers up would be dropped. We should bomb red markers if possible, if not then we should bomb the green markers. If there was cloud, we were to bomb the sky markers, which hung over the target at about 10,000 feet on parachutes for about a minute. The CO was followed by officers of the other trades. The navigator leader had a chart put up on the board that showed the position of all the squadron aircraft at the moment when they should have been crossing the enemy coast on the way out. A few were quite close but others were a long way out. He emphasized the importance of being on track and at the correct time, so that the concentration should be as great as possible, so as to swamp the defences. Safety in numbers.

The Germans had a defensive line arranged in boxes with a night fighter in each box. If we went through separated we could be picked off one at a time, but if we all bunched together most of us would get through in the crush. There were cheers from the crews who made a good showing, and groans from those who were badly off, then the CO and the station commander, Group Captain Crummy, made a few comments and that was it.

After the briefing we went back to the mess for the pre-flight meal. If you went on an op you were entitled to bacon and egg, which you could have before you went or when you came back. We always took it before we went to make sure we had it.

After collecting our gear and parachutes we were taken out to the plane, V Vic. It was about an hour before take-off, which gave us time to run up the engines and rectify any small snags such as a mag drop. There were no snags so we climbed out and larked about at the dispersal until it was time to go. The station commander and the squadron commander came round to check that everything was OK. As we were on the first wave we were among the first to start up and taxi out. As we taxied on to the runway I saw that there was a group of about fifty people waiting there to see us off, and I noticed my crew amongst them, no doubt hoping that they would be seeing me again shortly. I was too.

This was the first time I had taken off in a fully loaded Lancaster, and the difference was tremendous. We gathered speed very slowly and didn't lift off until we were doing about 100 knots, and the rate of climb was only about 200 feet per minute, with the engines at the maximum climb of 2,650 revs. The sky around us was filling up with other Lancasters slowly gaining height. Still, we got up to 10,000 feet and set course from over base, still climbing. At 14,000 feet we put the superchargers on to high speed as the boost was falling off. This enabled us to maintain our power to a greater altitude. For targets in northern Germany the point to cross the coast on the way out was at Mablethorpe, where all the aircraft of the group came together so as to be on the same track and achieve full concentration. The place was marked by a searchlight pointing vertically upwards, which we were able to see as it was getting dark. We set course across the North Sea, gradually gaining height until we got to 20,000 feet, when we could not climb any more. But we kept our revs at 2,650.

There was nothing for me to do except stand in the engineer's position beside the pilot and watch and learn. There was a Perspex bubble on the starboard side from where one could look straight down. The navigator was hard at work getting fixes on Gee, and giving alterations to the pilot as necessary to keep us on time and track so as to be in the middle of the stream. I had no idea what to expect when we got to the enemy coast, possibly some sort of action.

As we approached, tension on board increased and everybody's lookout sharpened. We just managed to make out the coast as we crossed it near Knocke in Belgium. It was a pitch black night with no cloud and we flew on seeing nothing, with about an hour to go to the target. We had to approach and bomb on an easterly course, then turn starboard twice and return. There was no sign of the target until about five minutes to zero hour when the sky ahead filled with twinkling flashes, rather like the Milky Way but in the wrong place. I was astonished and a bit apprehensive at the thought of having to fly through it but my hopes rose when I noticed that nobody else seemed a bit put out. I realized later, of course, that there was an optical illusion because all these bursts were situated over an area about ten miles apart and were no way near as dense as they appeared.

When we got to the target, however, there was a lot of activity: searchlights waving about, flares hanging low in the sky and TIs dropping and burning on the ground. From my position I had a good view below and could see bombs bursting, the cookies giving a huge flash, and the sticks of incendiaries leaving long streaks of light on the ground. As the target disappeared under the nose the bomb aimer called 'Bomb doors open.' Then shortly after, 'Left, left, left, left, bombs gone.' We felt the lurch when they left. We had to keep the plane level for a minute to take a photograph of the bomb burst, which seemed like an hour, but then it was 'Bomb doors shut' and we were free to manoeuvre if necessary.

The return to base was uneventful and I was reunited with my crew, all of us pleased. They wanted to know what it was like. 'Piece of cake,' I said.

As soon as we had finished debriefing, Flight Sergeant Wells was told that he had been screened. He had finished his tour and had no more trips to do, just the twenty-four. As a result, I was able to take over his plane V Vic, which had done twenty-four trips, and we did twenty-four more on it before it was damaged and returned to training duties. I saw it again a year later in the hangar at Hemswell, the Lancaster Finishing School.

Having done my second pilot trip, I was now fully operational, but there was one type of reasonably easy trip that they saved for the beginners. This was minelaying, codenamed *Gardening*, that is, planting vegetables.

This was what we did on our first trip by ourselves. Two days after my trip to Gelsenkirchen, on 27 June 1943, we were briefed to drop a load of mines at the mouth of the Gironde river where the passage narrows. There was a small island in

First Tour in 12 Squadron

the narrows that we had to locate, and then steer for thirty seconds from it on a course of 080 degrees.

We were then to drop the vegetables in a stick, dropping height 1,000 feet. The mines had parachutes to slow their descent. It sounded easy but was difficult to do on a pitch black night. There would be no cloud but no moon either.

We set off and crossed the Channel at 10,000 feet. Crossing the French coast did not seem as hostile as Germany. There was no activity and a complete blackout. We gently let down as we crossed France to 5,000 feet, then down to 1,000 when we approached the dropping zone. We could not see very much in the dark but were able to discern the coast and the narrow passage. However, we did not have much luck in locating the island. We circled around for several minutes searching, but fortunately there was not much enemy activity. Occasionally, a bit of light flak came up, looking like strings of about six light bulbs floating through the air. But, fortunately, they did not come anywhere near us. I don't think they saw us but were just firing so as to be observed doing their duty! Eventually we located the island, made our run, dropped the mines and headed for home. I often wonder whether those mines sank anything, but, altogether, the RAF minelaying was very successful. Anyway, the trip home was uneventful and the crew could chalk up our first op.

On 3 July we went on our first trip to Germany, to Cologne.

When we were getting dressed in the crew room I checked that everybody was OK. I said to Robbie, 'Everything ready Robbie?' 'Yes, all kitted up, right down to my fur-lined French letter.' It was bitterly cold at 20,000 feet and we needed to put on as much clothing as we could, especially the gunners. This did not apply to us all. There was a heating system operated from the engines that provided a little warm air but the outlets for this came out in the navigator's compartment so the navigator and radio operator were nice and warm but it was not so good up in the cockpit. I wore pyjamas under my trousers and long woollen sea boot stockings up to my knees with flying boots and silk gloves under leather ones.

At the briefing the intelligence officer said 'The target for tonight is Cologne and the aiming point is the square outside the cathedral. Marking will be by musical Oboe. Red TIs, with green backers up.' We were on the last wave, and as the weather was forecast to be cloudless with good visibility, finding the target should not be difficult. This turned out to be the case. We crossed the English coast at Beachy Head, which was standard for targets in the Ruhr, As we crossed the channel we were still climbing and were at 22,000 feet by the time we crossed the enemy coast at Knocke again.

In the distance ahead I could see what looked like a small lit up wigwam and as we got closer I realized that it was the target and saw the cone of searchlights over it. Our track was to pass to the south of Cologne, then turn port and bomb on a northerly heading. After bombing, we were to turn starboard and starboard again, then a third turn would bring us back home on a similar track. The target was similar to what I had seen at Gelsenkirchen, with lots of light and scattered flak, which didn't worry us.

We dropped our bombs at the right time in the middle of our wave – the target was a mass of flames below. As pilot, I was not able to see it as the plane blocked my view, but I could see the glow beneath us.

After bombing and doing our two ninety-degree turns to starboard, we could see the target on our starboard beam. There was a late arrival on his bombing run, flying slightly higher than us. The flak barrage had stopped, and the other plane was coned in the searchlights. There was a wait of a few seconds then a burst of lots of flak around him and he burst into flames and went down. 'So much for flak accuracy falling off above 18,000 feet,' I thought, with memories of the talk at

First Tour in 12 Squadron

Hixon by the Army officer. I knew now that it was fatal to get anywhere by yourself. However, the general barrage flak never worried me as they could not concentrate their fire on any particular plane, but just had to blast away at random into the sky. But as soon as a plane was coned they could do so. The trip home was uneventful and that was number three under my belt.

On 8 July we did another trip to Cologne, more or less the same as before, but got up to 22,500 feet this time. I was beginning to adjust to the pattern of these raids. There was not constant flak all the way to the target; all the searchlights and flak were congregated over the towns. In between was relatively quiet, but of course that was the area where the night fighters operated. I knew that these fighters were guided on to us by radar, and that the range at which they could actually see you and open fire was very short, a few hundred yards. Also, if they lost you it was difficult to find you again quickly. I estimated that the time from when they first picked you up on radar until they opened fire was about fifteen minutes. So what you had to do was to change your lateral position slightly. I devised what I called 'the Rowland turn', which consisted of a left hand rate one turn through ninety degrees followed by a right turn to the right, which brought you back to your original course but a mile to one side. Fifteen minutes later you did it again but the opposite way round, thus bringing you back to your original track, but having lost a minute of travel. It would be very difficult for a fighter to follow this and it was easy for the navigator to cope with. I tried this out successfully a few times but in view of the risk of collision from other aircraft in the bomber stream, I gave up as I was changing one danger for another. After all, one would not survive a collision but could perhaps get away with a tangle with a fighter. So we concentrated on keeping a very good lookout. It was an unfortunate fact that with the fighter approaching slightly below you, it was difficult to see him against the dark ground, while he could more easily pick you up against the sky. I only wished that we had a more experienced rear gunner.

We always tried to get as much height as possible. Maximum continuous revs for the Merlins was 2,650 revs, which was the standard climbing revs, so we just kept on climbing until we climbed no more but kept the revs at 2,650. As time passed and we used up fuel and our weight slowly dropped, we seemed to gain a little height but not very much. We were usually briefed to maintain our bombing height for the journey home, so instead of climbing higher we were able to reduce our revs. By then our weight had gone down a lot by dropping our bombs.

The Merlins were remarkably reliable and were able to stand a bit of a beating. We had one pilot who did not take off until just before the final time he was allowed. He was so far behind the rest of the main force that he kept his engines at 2,850, the maximum take-off revs, all the way to the target, with no appreciable problem, though the aircraft needed a thorough overhaul after he landed.

When we crossed the enemy coast at about 20,000 feet, the tension on board tended to increase a little. It is not a very pleasant experience to fly along in the dark expecting a cannon shell up your backside at any moment, though strangely enough you grew accustomed to it. But it never became a pleasure! There was plenty to do to keep your mind occupied, with everybody on the alert and keeping a good lookout. There was one aid to help keep us safe, a device called Boozer. This was a radar receiver set that was directed backwards and tuned to the frequency of the German night fighter frequency. When it picked up a signal a little red light lit up on the instrument panel. That was all the indication that it gave, (no range or anything like that). It was just a warning that a fighter was after you. The light came on for a few seconds quite frequently and sent my blood pressure up a bit but nearly always went out pretty quickly. I remember on one occasion on a very dark night over northern France the light stayed on so I took a little evasive action, with no effect, then did an orbit. In the middle of this a small plane went over us and the light went out. Thank you, Boozer. It was after this that I invented my Rowland turn.

On 9 July there was also a bit of good luck. I was walking through the camp when I came across Sergeant Pete Lyons, the rear gunner we had lost at Lindholme. 'What are you doing here?' I asked him. He said he had been put in another crew and they had been posted to 12 Squadron. We discussed the chance of his coming back to us. I went to see the CO and put the position to him, and he said we could do it if the other pilot did not mind. The other pilot did not mind as he was only changing one gunner, not well known to him, for another he did not know. So Pete was back with us, much to our delight. He moved into the same hut as the rest of the crew, complete with his large collection of gramophone records, a great asset.

We went to Gelsenkirchen that night, 9 July, very happy with our new rear gunner, but it was very different to my previous trips as the weather was very cloudy with poor visibility. As we approached the target, we were still in cloud at 23,000 feet. When our time came near, Derrick, the navigator, said 'What shall we do?' With a couple of minutes to go, I opened the bomb doors and replied 'We'll drop them on ETA.' There was a gruff shout from Ken, the bomb aimer. 'I'm not letting my bombs go unless I can see some TIs.' Just after he spoke there was a group of flashes of flak just off the starboard wing. 'Bombs gone,' said Ken and we felt them go. We saw no more flak and did not get out of the cloud until we were well on the way home. It was very disappointing, and the only time I dropped my bombs in cloud. There were few losses that night and the squadron didn't lose any; perhaps the night fighters had trouble in the cloud too!

After the second trip to Cologne, Charlie was promoted to warrant officer. This gave him immense prestige as, in the RAF, warrant officers are only slightly below God. Some of this also added to the standing of the crew, what with me being a flight lieutenant, as most crews consisted of pilot officers and sergeants only.

I got into the habit of going in the evenings to the crew's Nissen hut where we played cribbage and listened to Pete's extensive record collection. Paddy used to bring us refreshments late at night, for which he used to help himself to stocks of tea and sugar from the cook house. Unfortunately, this became so bad that it came to the notice of the service police who decided to carry out a search of all the NCOs' huts. Paddy fortunately got wind of this and very cleverly hid his stocks in Charlie's bed. The police arrived and in Paddy's presence started to search the various beds. When they were about to search Charlie's bed, Paddy called out, 'That's Warrant Officer Edwards's bed. He'll be furious if he finds out you've been going through his things.' This stopped the police in their tracks and they retreated hastily, so our hot refreshments late at night continued.

On 25 July, when we got back from a week's leave, Essen was the next trip – No. 6. It was a bit of a scare when we saw the target at briefing as it had a reputation as being very difficult target to hit because of the industrial haze surrounding it, a result of it being right in the middle of the Ruhr. But it turned out to be not too bad despite its reputation as a difficult target. We were on the last wave and bombed from 21,000 feet. When we dropped our bombs we seemed to be about halfway up the column of black smoke rising from

First Tour in 12 Squadron

it. The use of Oboe had obviously ended the problem of hitting Essen.

On 26 July the battle of Hamburg started. I was not on that night, but I was given the task of going round every plane before take-off to ensure that every bomb aimer was fully cognizant of the way he should use the new device called Window. This was a small strip of metallic paper about four inches long and an inch wide. It was made up in bundles of about a hundred that had to be put down a chute in the bomb aimer's position at the rate of one every minute. When these strips hit the slipstream they burst and formed a cloud, which gave a similar radar response to an aircraft. This meant that the radar screens of the Germans would be swamped with echoes so that individual aircraft could not be identified. When our planes got back it turned out that Window had been a great success and losses were very low.

I was put on the next night, 27 July, but at the briefing I was staggered to find that we had been put in the first wave. As this was only our seventh trip I had not been expecting this. From now on we could not see the target from twenty minutes away but would have to get there without any outside guidance. But with confidence in my navigator I was quite sure that we would manage it. We set off and at zero hour minus two minutes we were at 21,000 feet in pitch darkness. Not a searchlight, flare or TI. I asked Derrick, 'Are you sure we're in the right place?' He replied, 'Yes we're bang on.' I opened the bomb doors just in case. A few seconds later, Ken shouted out 'Green TIs just under the nose!' Then, 'Bombs gone.' Seconds later all hell was let loose – dozens of searchlights and lots of flak. I kept the aircraft steady for the photograph and kept going, soon disappearing into the dark beyond the target, leaving chaos behind us. We had no trouble on the way home, and when we saw our photograph the next day we saw quite plainly the Blohm and Voss shipyard in the middle of Hamburg so we had got the aiming point. It was undoubtedly a magnificent piece of navigation by Derrick.

We went to Hamburg again on 29 July, this time on the last wave. We did not know it at the time but these raids were so successful that they caused the catastrophic fire storms that consumed large parts of the city.

On 30 July we went to Remscheid. This was a small town east of Cologne where they manufactured specialist steel, rather like Sheffield. At the briefing we were told that the route to the target was to pass beyond Cologne to the south, then turn back and bomb from the east on a westerly heading. Then we were to pass through the gap in the defences between Cologne and Dusseldorf. This time, instead of coming home at 20,000 feet, we should climb as high as possible as far as the enemy coast.

I had noticed at briefing that the wave behind us consisted of Stirlings. I knew that they had a very poor ceiling, about 15,000 feet. I therefore said to the navigator, 'I want to fall back until we are in their time zone, so I want us to bomb a bit late.' 'OK,' he replied. After we had bombed a minute or so late, and were on the way home, we saw in front of us a huge wall of searchlights with several Lancasters coned and being shelled heavily. Then just as we got to them, all the lights suddenly came down and coned several Stirlings well below us, and we sailed through above them untroubled in the dark. We kept climbing, and with no bombs and a lot of our fuel used up we got up to 25,000 feet. We had an uneventful flight home, though it was bitterly cold, 25 degrees below I seem to remember.

We were briefed again to go to Hamburg on 2 August, this time on the last wave again. Halfway across the North Sea I was surprised to see flashes in the sky ahead and thought this must be the Hamburg flak in action. But when we got to the

First Tour in 12 Squadron

enemy coast I discovered that it was lightning. The thunderstorms were all around us. As we got closer, and as there didn't seem to be any other way around, we went straight in to one of them at 20,000 feet.

Once we were in the cloud, the conditions were atrocious, with continuous flashes of lightning, though we were not struck by it. There was also dreadful turbulence. After a minute I realized that there was no future in carrying on and turned round and came out of it. Apparently, another pilot in the squadron, Sergeant Curry, also went in and got out of control, losing his ailerons before he managed to recover. He did well to get back to base and land without further damage. After getting back to clear air we managed to get round the cloud but did not find any sign of an attack taking place, so we finished up dropping our bombs on some fires on the ground. That was the end of the battle of Hamburg.

Window proved to be so effective that it completely destroyed the Kammhuber Line system, also known as the Himmelbett. This resulted in the Germans devising a new system, which turned out to be much better than the old one. This was called *Wilde Sau* (Wild Boar). Under this system they created radio beacons all over Germany. The German fighters would wait at one of these beacons. Then when the controllers had located the bomber stream they would tell the fighter to fly to another one, and hope and expect that the course they were flying would take them through the stream. Then they could follow the stream and use their airborne radar sets to locate and destroy their targets, of which there would be many around them. This system worked extremely well, and some fighter pilots succeeded in shooting down several planes in one night. One German pilot that I met after the war claimed to have shot down six on the night when the RAF went to Nuremberg and lost ninety-six.

Another nasty trick the *Luftwaffe* developed was to install cannons firing vertically upwards so that they could attack from below where they were not easily seen.

Another *Luftwaffe* development was that a German pilot, Major Hajo Hermann, persuaded Goering to allow him to form a unit that flew single-seater fighters to operate at night with the object of attacking bombers over the target while they were illuminated by the searchlights. They had a fair bit of success and I came into contact with one of them myself at a later date.

We did not operate for five days then had a nice trip on 7 August to bomb Genoa. It was a long way to go across France and the Alps. There was very little opposition over the target, but Charlie had a good view of the port and claimed to have had a sight of a battleship. Having done a tour in Coastal Command, he expected to be believed, but the debriefing officer took no notice. The flying time was nine hours exactly; luckily I had my little bottle with me!

One of the problems that I had was my bladder. With the length of the flights we were doing I nearly always eventually found myself in extreme discomfort. There was an Elsan at the back of the fuselage and the other members of the crew were able to go and make use of it. But this method was no good for me, as I did not like the idea of leaving the controls on autopilot, unattended, while I went a long way away. The solution was to take some kind of bottle, but finding a suitable one was a problem. However, I found the answer when I came across the bottle in which Essolube oil was sold. This was large enough and also had a fairly large neck opening, which exactly fitted a Thermos flask cork. I then got into the habit of filling the bottle about five minutes before we reached the target. I then handed it down to the bomb aimer who put it through a little hatch so that it rested on the bomb doors. Then when I opened the bomb doors the bottle fell on to the target. So I can claim that in addition to the bombs many German towns have had the benefit of a bottle of Rowland's best.

After Italy it was back to the tough targets in Germany. It was Mannheim on 9 August. There was plenty of activity over the target. I can remember the sight of a load of incendiaries dropping from a Lancaster ahead and a bit above us. In the light from the searchlights it looked just like a waterfall. We were at 20,000 feet and had no trouble on the way home, touching down after six and a quarter hours.

The next day we did the first of our three trips to Nuremberg, a slightly longer flight of seven and a half hours. This was a very poor attack; the TIs were very scattered as Nuremberg was a difficult target for the Pathfinders to find. We were out of range of Oboe, and they had to rely on H2S. During the bomb run there was a lot of chatter on the intercom and Pete complained about this after we landed. I said that the bomb aimer had to give his directions. Pete said 'What if I see a fighter and have to warn you?' 'Well, if you can't make yourself heard you'll just have to shoot it out with him.' Fortunately, it never came to that.

We had a week off then as it was full moon, but on 17 August we were briefed for Peenemunde. This was an experimental station on the Baltic coast, and we had to bomb from 6,000 feet. We had to cross Denmark at 10,000 feet, then let down to the target. It was so important that if it was not destroyed we would have to keep returning to it until it was. This didn't seem too attractive.

As we approached the Danish coast at 10,000 feet it was bright moonlight, almost like day. Suddenly Pete called up 'The rear turret is US (unserviceable).' This was the second time this had happened and seriously hampered his ability to keep a lookout. At that moment another plane was shot down just to starboard of us. I called to Robbie to keep an extra good lookout as Pete's turret was US. There was no reply and the wireless operator called up 'He's not in his turret, he's gone back to help Pete.' 'Christ, what a cock up,' I thought and wondered what we should do. I called up everybody in turn to ask them but nobody wanted to give a decision. Last of all I asked Charlie, and he said 'Let's bugger off home.' 'What shall we do with the bombs?' I asked the bomb aimer. He said 'It looks like a flare path just below.' Derrick said that would be Sylt so we dropped our bombs on it and went home.

We heard later that the raid was a great success, and I regret that we were not able to take part. But I believe it was the right decision, as there were a lot of losses near the target from fighters, and without our turret we would have been easy meat. But I should have made the decision myself, and not asked the crew. As we had dropped our bombs on enemy soil the trip counted for us, so it was a very easy one.

On 22 August the target was Leverkusen, just across the Rhine from Cologne, but unlike the Cologne attacks it was a complete shambles. The marking was poor, the TIs very scattered and there was no concentration of bombing at all.

At the briefing the next day, 23 August, we had a shock to see the target – Berlin. We were told that there was a new tactic to be used. A master bomber. This was one of the Pathfinders who would call up on the RT and give corrections to the TIs if necessary. We had to keep our sets on over the target so that we could hear him.

We had an untroubled trip to the target. When we got there we could see that things were very scattered. I heard a very English voice say 'Come on in chaps, there's nothing to worry about. Bomb the green TIs.' Then a very Australian voice said 'Why don't you f—k off home.' We bombed from 21,000 feet. After that the trip was uneventful.

First Tour in 12 Squadron

An old acquaintance now turned up in B Flight, Flight Lieutenant Haydn Goule. He had been a pupil on the instructors' course at the Central Flying School. I had not been his instructor but I had been aware of his presence as he was a very forceful man and always very anxious that everybody should know that he had been an operational pilot, of which he was very proud. He had now turned up to do his second tour. He was Welsh like me and lived in Barry in South Wales, very close to where my parents were living in Bonvilston. We became very good friends and when we went on leave at the same time I gave him a lift in my car. I drove him to Barry first, where he introduced me to his family and girlfriend and he persuaded me to go on a bit of a night out before I went home.

I very thoughtlessly agreed and after an enjoyable evening went to where my parents were living in a flat in a large country house that the county council had commandeered and in which he had a flat as being the county ex-officio Air Raid Precautions head man. I drove on to the drive. All the lights were off and when I arrived an upstairs window opened and my mother looked out and in a very tearful voice said 'Who is that?' 'Me of course,' I replied, much to her delight. They had been expecting me on leave and when it was announced by the BBC that there had been a big raid on Germany the previous night and a lot of aircraft missing, they had assumed the worst when I did not turn up. I felt very bad at my thoughtlessness. However, all was forgiven. I have to give credit to my parents who had the worry all through the war of my being in the RAF. The worry became worse when my brother was out in India and Burma, but fortunately we both came through unscathed.

In the middle of August Wing Commander Woods finished his tour and we got a new commanding officer. This was Wing Commander Towle, a very different kettle of fish to

Return Flights in War and Peace

Woods. He had no operational experience at all. I think he had spent his war up until then flying a desk in Whitehall. We all wanted to see what he would do as he was not in a position to take a new crew as Woods had done. He sent us off on a few trips and at briefing it was obvious that he didn't have a clue about anything. At length, on 29 August it was announced that he was going as second pilot that night with Flight Lieutenant Booth who was doing his twenty-fourth trip and was considered one of the top pilots in the squadron. When we heard the news we all said to each other, 'It must be an easy one tonight.' Sure enough, when we got to the briefing we found that the target was Munchengladbach, a town just west of the Ruhr. We did not have to penetrate the Ruhr defences very far to get there and we felt rather happy about it. We looked forward to a trip with few losses. This was my eighteenth trip.

When we got back we were able to report at debriefing that we had not seen anybody shot down but to our surprise there was no sign of Flight Lieutenant Booth's plane. The final result was that we only lost two planes that night and one of them carried our new boss, which goes to show that a bullet will get you if your name is on it!

A few days later his replacement arrived, a Wing Commander Craven, who turned out quite satisfactory, though no one could be up to Woods' standard in our opinion. I personally had nothing against him as he recommended me for my DFCs and very kindly gave me an exceptional assessment at the end of my tour.

On 27 August it was Nuremberg again and another very poor attack. We were on the last wave again and bombed from 21,000 feet on to a very scattered target. Nuremberg was out of range of Oboe so the marking was done by Pathfinders who had to locate the target by H2S, illuminate it by strings of flares, then try to identify the aiming point visually – a very

First Tour in 12 Squadron

difficult task. Also, it was a very miserable trip for Pete as the rear turret was US again and he had to operate it by hand, which was very tiring.

Next day, I flew down to Wittering in the group captain's Tiger Moth to fetch Wally Snell. He had had a most amazing experience the night before. The route to Nuremberg had necessitated leaving England at Beachy Head. This meant an alteration of course of about 80 degrees to port from flying down from Lincolnshire due south on 180 degrees, then at the turning point turning port on to 100 for the crossing to France. His bomb aimer was lying in the bomb aimer's position on his stomach, with the intention of telling the navigator when they were at Beachy Head when another Lancaster, who was not keeping a very good look out, passed across on the new course so close below that the tip of his port tail fin knocked off the pitot head (airspeed indicator) of Wally's plane. This stuck out about a foot below from the front of a Lancaster. As Wally had no ASI now he was not able to carry on to Nuremberg so he had to jettison his cookie in the North Sea as landing with it on was prohibited. There were several emergency airfields specially for this sort of emergency. Wittering was one of them. It had an enormously long grass runway where two grass fields about a mile apart had been connected up to form one long one. With no airspeed indicator it was impossible to check your speed on the approach so you had to come in very fast so as to make sure not to stall. Even without the cookie, but with most of his fuel and the rest of the bomb load, the plane was still very heavy and landing back at base would have been impossible. Flying the Tiger Moth after the Lancaster was an enjoyable change with the open cockpit and all.

We went on leave in September and didn't fly again until 22 September when we did my first trip to Hanover. But this trip was very different for me. I had done eighteen trips by then so was selected to take a new crew on their first trip. Unlike my own first trip when I went as a passenger, in this case I took the whole new crew, but as was customary I took my own navigator, as one didn't want to risk taking a new one.

The pilot in question was Sergeant Ellis. We bombed from 20,000 feet on the first wave. The target was well defended, and I saw a Lancaster shot down over the target by a fighter while it was coned. Sergeant Ellis went on to be a very successful pilot and was awarded the CGM (Conspicuous Gallantry Medal), a very rare distinction.

Taking a new crew meant that my own crew fell another trip behind me as they had already lost one when I did my first as a passenger. Pilots were screened after they had done thirty trips. The crew members were usually screened as well unless they were a few behind, in which case they were kept on to do a few more as spare bods, something that was a very unpopular fate.

On 27 September it was Hanover again. We bombed from 19,000 feet on the first wave. It was quite a good attack but the marking was not too good so it was a bit scattered.

On 29 September we went to Bochum and on 1 October to Hagen. They were two towns in the Ruhr where we were again in range of Oboe, so we had good results as a result.

The disadvantage with having Charlie as an engineer was that he had done a tour in Coastal Command and so was now on his second tour, so he would be eligible to finish after twenty trips with us. We had been jollying him along that he would carry on with us to the end. But he resolutely, and quite rightly, said that he would finish after his twentieth.

He was two behind me. Hagen was my twenty-second trip and as Charlie was two behind it was his last. From then on we had several new crew members.

First Tour in 12 Squadron

Up until then we had had a fairly trouble-free tour, but our luck must have gone with Charlie as from then on it was very different.

The next day we went to Munich, with Sergeant Macey as engineer. It was a pretty long flight of eight and a quarter hours. We flew all the way along Lake Constance then turned port to approach the target on a northerly heading. As we neared Munich the searchlights were very active and at length one latched on to us. In a few seconds others joined them and we were well and truly coned. This meant that the flak could concentrate on us. When the flak had a target it took thirty seconds for them to do their calculations, set the shell fuse, load and fire, and the shell to come up and burst in the position where they calculated the plane would be by then. The secret was to alter course and or height so as to make sure that you were somewhere else, and then carry on jinking in this way until you eventually got out of range of the searchlights, which could not follow you very far. The seconds passed and just at the moment when I was expecting the flak to arrive, everything went bright red around us. For a split second I believed I was dead, but a second or so later the lights went out and we were flying in the dark. I looked behind us and saw that the flak had scored a direct hit on a Lancaster flying a hundred yards behind us and exploded. We flew on with my heart beating a little fast, dropped our bombs on the target at 20,000 feet and went home with no further trouble.

I realized later that the reason the lights had gone out was because the Lancaster that the flak had hit was so close to us that they thought they had got their target so went off to find a new one.

This also confirmed my opinion that there was no such a thing as a 'Scarecrow'.

Return Flights in War and Peace

This was an idea that had been put about that there was something that the Germans were putting up that looked like an exploding aircraft, with the intention of affecting morale. I considered this to be nonsense. If the biggest gun that the Germans had, fired the biggest shell it could fire to 20,000 feet and it looked like a flash for a second, how on earth could they get something up there that looked like the explosion of 1,500 gallons of petrol and five tons of explosive? No, it was an aircraft exploding, and now I had seen one at close quarters I knew that aircraft did explode.

After the war the Germans admitted that they had never heard of Scarecrows and had certainly never fired anything of that type. A possible solution to this belief came later when we found out about the German development of mounting cannons in the night fighters, pointing vertically upwards. They very cleverly did not use incendiary ammunition in them so that it was some time before we found about it. It was called *Schräge Musik*. They were able to creep up below the bomber where they could not be seen and destroy the aircraft without any sign of a combat by any other nearby bombers. If the victim exploded it would have looked exactly the same as a so-called Scarecrow.

Two days later, we went to Frankfurt. We had a new engineer, Sergeant Randall, who stayed with us to the end of the tour. We were on the third wave and bombed from 19,000 feet. It was another Pathfinder-marked raid, but another bad trip for Pete as the turret was US again and we were getting a bit fed up with this recurring fault. So when on 7 October we were on the way to Stuttgart and the rear turret was US again we turned back and came home, jettisoning the cookie in the North Sea and bringing the rest home.

The next day, 8 October, disaster struck. We were on the way to Hanover and half an hour from the target at 20,000 feet. It was pitch black and half a dozen or so flares appeared,

First Tour in 12 Squadron

hanging above and ahead of us. I took this to be fighter activity and warned every one to keep an extra good lookout. A few minutes later Pete shouted out 'Fighter, starboard go.' I immediately started to put the starboard wing down, but had not got far into the turn when a line of tracer cannon shells, looking like light bulbs, went past the window and there was a thud from somewhere in the fuselage. I knew from my experience with the Rowland turn that we would have lost the fighter, and we never saw him again. I then called up all the crew in turn to check how they were. They were all OK except there was no reply from Pete. I told the engineer to get a portable oxygen bottle and go back and check. A few minutes later he called back to say that Pete had been killed by a cannon shell that had hit the turret. I asked if he could get Pete out of the turret but he said 'no' so he came back up to the front.

We were only a few minutes from the target by then and there seemed no point in turning back so we carried on and bombed. We felt a bit vulnerable on the way home with only one gunner to keep a lookout, but fortunately we ran into no more trouble.

When we arrived back at base I called up 'Ambulance needed' and we got immediate permission to land, but when we were down it became obvious that there was nothing to be done.

I have often thought about this attack. Since the war I have attended several German night fighter reunions and have spoken to many of their pilots. They all tell me that they were very chary of firing at the fuselage of Lancasters on the way to the target as with the bomb load on board there was a risk of an explosion, which might engulf them as well. They would therefore aim at the wing between the inner and outer engines where the fuel tanks were. There was also the fact that the crew had a better chance of getting away with it alive, which they said gave them a good feeling! This fitted in with what I had experienced, as I had not got very far into the turn when they fired, but putting down the wing caused the fire to miss the tanks and pass over the wing.

A day never passes that I do not thank Pete for giving me an extra sixty years of life. It was a tragedy that he lost his life while saving the lives of the rest of us. It was pitch black at the time and how he managed to see the fighter I cannot understand. We have just had a memorial tree planted for him at Wickenby.

We had a week's leave after Pete's death, during which we went to his funeral in Gillingham in Kent, where we met his family. Funerals in Bomber Command were not very usual as most missing planes just didn't come back and we didn't know what had happened to them. If we were lucky we found out that the crew were prisoners of war, though this did not happen very often.

When we got back we went to Hanover again, but we had a nice new aircraft, ED359. Our old Lancaster, W4990, was too badly damaged to stay on the squadron; it needed a new rear turret, which necessitated a trip back to a maintenance unit. It had done forty-eight trips, which was quite a big number in those days, although later in the war when the trips were a lot easier, several did over 100. But with plenty of new planes available, with up-to-date modifications, such as H2S, she was not up to present requirements. She had plenty of life left in her and was pensioned off to a training role. I saw her a year later in the hangar at Hemswell working for the Lancaster Finishing School.

Once again, I was chosen to take a new pilot and crew. He was a Sergeant Birchall and I took my own navigator as usual. I also took my own mid-upper gunner, Sergeant Robinson, because his wife had been sick and he had lost a couple of trips while on compassionate leave. This had put him a few

First Tour in 12 Squadron

behind me and so he didn't want to lose another and run the risk of having to stay on as a spare bod when the rest of us finished. With the new crew, we were on the last wave and approaching the target. The ground was obscured by ten-tenths low cloud, and with the incendiaries burning below it the result was that it was nearly as bright as day.

Suddenly, I heard a scream on the intercom and I immediately shoved the stick forward. We dropped and as we did a burst of fire came over my head and shattered the windscreen. I started to corkscrew and then as I straightened up I found that there was a fighter fifty yards ahead of me. To my amazement it was a single-seater, a Messerschmitt 109. He had obviously attacked us in a dive faster than us and when I dived we disappeared out of his sight under his nose. He had carried on and finished ahead of us, which would not have happened to a twin-engined fighter. I could see him quite clearly but he had obviously lost sight of us and started weaving gently from side to side. I shouted to the bomb aimer, who doubled as front gunner, to get in the front turret and shoot him down. He acknowledged and then I heard no more as he disconnected his intercom to move to a new position. Seconds passed, which seemed like minutes, but nothing happened so I told Birchall to go and chivvy him up. A few seconds later the bomb aimer came back on the intercom and said 'I can't get the sight on.' I replied, 'Fire without it, you can't miss him at this range.' I saw a short burst of tracer that went nowhere near him. He must have seen it for he turned on his back and headed down vertically and I never saw him again. What a missed opportunity to shoot down a fighter from the front turret of a Lancaster. Almost unique.

I have thought about this a lot since and realize that the blame was not with the bomb aimer but with me. It was his first trip and while we were crossing the North Sea I should have made him get in the turret and test his guns, something that my own bomber Ken would have done as a matter of course.

We were at the edge of the target area so we went on and dropped our bombs from 21,000 feet. We had had a fair sprinkle of fire so once we were out of the target I sent the engineer back to check the gunner. He called up that the gunner had been hit in the head by a bullet. He had got him out of his turret, put him on the rest bed and given him some morphine. The return journey was completed without further incident and again on arrival at Wickenby I called for an ambulance. When we touched down I found that we had a flat tyre with the result that we swung off the runway and finished on the grass. This was lucky as the runway was not obstructed and the rest of the squadron were not delayed. The ambulance soon arrived and we put Robbie in it. While they were doing this, Birchall said to me, 'I think there's something in my back.' I stood behind him and after he had pulled up his shirt I saw what appeared to be some sort of a puncture in his back. When I showed this to the ambulance men they took him off with them to hospital. It transpired later that it was a bullet wound, and the bullet had lodged in his lung.

This resulted in his being taken off flying and he never flew again. He therefore had a very short career in Bomber Command.

The flight engineer had had a very narrow escape. His task was to keep a lookout of the Perspex bubble on the starboard side of the fuselage, just above the engineer's panel. Just before we were attacked he told me that he had to take his half-hourly readings so he sat down at the panel. When we inspected the Perspex later we saw that there was a small hole in the front of the bubble and another in the back. If his head had been in the bubble the bullet would have gone in at one ear and out of the other. So ended the second exciting trip in succession.

A fortnight later, on 3 November, it was back to the Ruhr with a trip to Dusseldorf, my twenty-seventh trip. With our new plane we got up to bomb from 22,000 feet. We had a new mid-upper gunner, Flight Sergeant Risi. He and Sergeant Randall stayed with us for the rest of our tour. They were both 'odd bods' who had had to stay on when their crews finished.

About now my flight commander, Squadron Leader Heyworth, finished his tour and I was hoping to be promoted in his place. When I spoke to the CO he said that as I only had a few trips left it was not worth me getting the post and he promoted my very great friend Flight Lieutenant Haydn Goule instead, although he was considerably junior to me. Poor Haydn was shot down and killed on a trip to Berlin in January 1944.

Shortly after his promotion, Haydn took me aside and told me that I had been recommended for a DFC. This was a great surprise to me as I had not been expecting it, though I found out later that things in Bomber Command at that time were so bad that nearly all pilots who finished a tour received that decoration. It came through just before I finished my tour.

On 10 November we were briefed for a nice easy trip to the south of France to a place called Modane. This was a railway station at the mouth of the tunnel to Italy. It was hoped that bombing it would block the tunnel and prevent re-enforcements from Germany getting through. Defences were expected to be light.

I was in the first wave. I was selected to hang around the target to assess the results and send in a report to Group. It turned out that there was no opposition at all. The bombing was very poor, with no heavy flak at all. After landing, at the debrief I said there was no opposition and a lot of the bombs were landing in the mountains around the target and doing not much except melting the snow.

The intelligence officer refuted this and said that there was a lot of flak and that the reports were that the bombing was very accurate, and that Group would not like it. However, I insisted on sending in my report as stated, and the next day after reconnaissance photos had been studied they said that I had been correct. I believe that a lot of inexperienced crews had mistaken the flare flashes that we had dropped for flak.

The next day I heard that I had been screened together with all my crew, although I had only done twenty-eight trips. I had also been promoted to squadron leader as a flight commander at 1656 HCU at Lindholme.

Chapter 13

Back at Lindholme

So I was back at Lindholme as a squadron leader after two years and four months as a flight lieutenant. I was OC A Flight, with five instructors under me and five Halifaxes. The pupils were qualified pilots and their crews had to be shown how to fly in four-engined aircraft. After the pilot had gone solo, they did a six-hour cross-country over the Irish Sea, as well as local circuits and landings at night. They did not come as a course but operated singly, going on to the Lancaster flight when they were ready.

I had only been there a few days when I had the shock of my life. I went into the anteroom in the officers' mess and picked up *The Times*. I looked first at the casualty lists, which were published regularly. Then, out of curiosity, I looked at the decoration list and to my amazement saw that I had been awarded a bar to my DFC.

The maintenance at Lindholme was not very good, and sometimes we had the crews coming back to the office saying the aircraft had a fault and was US. As a result it was difficult to complete our flying programme. One day a new engineer officer arrived and we were called in to the group captain's office to hear his plan. All the aircraft would be in his charge. The problem was that the maintenance crews were snowed in by having unserviceable aircraft returned to them, which they were too busy to deal with. Under the new system we would have two serviceable aircraft allotted to us and if they went US they would be replaced by another. As he said, although two didn't sound much it was better than having six US ones. In the event, the system worked very well and our flying times rose as our frustration fell.

Another reason that the flying times rose was because of an idea that I had. I thought to myself, 'If I'm only to have two aeroplanes, I may as well make the flying day a bit longer.' So I detailed one instructor and one pupil crew to start work in the morning so that they could take off at 7 o'clock. This was not very well received by the people concerned, but as I lay in bed the next morning at 7 o'clock I heard the sound of a Halifax taking off. Everybody noticed this, of course, and it was not long before the other flight was doing the same. The station commander was pleased as well.

I didn't do much flying myself as my job was doing the organizing, which suited me as I hated the Halifax which I considered dangerous and a great let down after flying Lancasters.

One fault that they had was that the flap lever and the undercart lever were side by side and identical, so it was easy to pull up the wrong one. This was carefully explained to the pupils as it could be very dangerous. When in the air the flaps had to be raised a little at a time, otherwise if they were raised in one go the plane dropped a hundred feet or so until it gained sufficient speed to manage without them. This applied to all aircraft with flaps; it was just that in the Halifax it was easy to pull the wrong lever. In the Lancaster one was a lever but the other was a ring that you pulled, so it was difficult to use the wrong one. The situation when this was most important was if you had a baulked landing and had to open up and go round again at full throttle with wheels and flaps down at fifty feet or so.

One day a new instructor arrived in my flight who had done a tour in Halifaxes, so the flying was easy for him. Soon

B Squadron new arrivals at Cranwell. Author at left end of front row.

The author in the cockpit of a Hawker Hind.

The trusty Alvis.

John at Cranwell.

The Cranwell course out on the tarmac.

OBLIQUE SIGHTING - HECTOR.

The Oblique Sighting equipment as viewed from the cockpit of a Hector.

The principle of the range and direction reporting system.

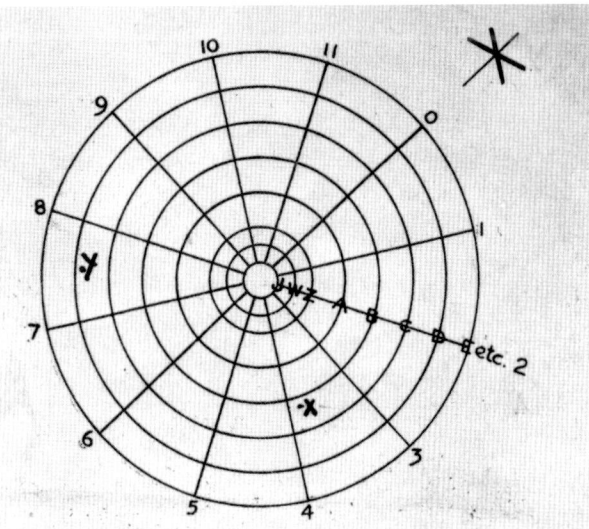

The distances of the circles, in yards, from the centre of the clock are as follows :—

J	W	Z	A	B	C	D	E	F	G	H	I	M	N
10	25	50	100	200	300	400	500	600	700	800	900	1000	1500

In addition, the letter Y is used for any distance over 1500 yards.

John flying a Hawker Hind at Cranwell.

A group of 613 Squadron pilots.

The airfield at Netherthorpe from the air.

A Westland Lysander army co-operation aircraft.

A painting by Peter Haughton of Hawker Hector K8108 that the author flew to attack Calais in May 1940.

Lysanders at dispersal at Firbeck.

Tiger Houghton shaving outside his tent in the grounds of the manor at Netherthorpe.

The author stands by a Lysander at Old Sarum.

Tiger and the author on the promenade at Weston.

A group of 12 Squadron prisoners of war.

The author and his wife with Bonnie the dog when newly married.

Martin Becker, Luftwaffe night fighter ace; he scored 58 victories and was awarded the Knight's Cross. He shot down six Lancasters on the author's bad night over Nurenburg.

Night Fighter Ace Hauptmann Walter Ehle, the Gruppenkommandereur of II/NJG standing in front of his Me 110.

A series of German 88 mm anti-aircraft guns firing in unison.

A Flak emplacement in Hamburg with three 88 mm guns.

A German Flak searchlight.

A British bomber lies destroyed in front of a battery of German anti-aircraft 88s.

On the left John's Distinguished Flying Cross and Bar and on the right his Distinguished Service Order.

Squadron Leader John Rowland DSO, DFC* shortly before leaving RAF service.

An AVRO York in Cosford Aviation Museum.

Memories! John leans from the cockpit of Lancaster *Just Jane* when he was at the Heroes' Day book signing at East Kirkby.

Comrades in arms – John, Charlie and Robbie at the reunion at Wickenby.

John stands before the preserved Lancaster at East Kirkby in September 2005.

BACK AT LINDHOLME

after, he was put on the night flying programme. This consisted of three instructors taking three pupils in turn until each was ready to go solo, after which they had to do three circuits and landings solo, by which time they were fully qualified, day and night. I was not on the programme myself, and when I arrived at the flight in the morning I discovered that the worst had happened. While giving dual to one of the crews he had to go round again and apparently the flaps had been pulled up at fifty feet and the plane had dropped on to the ground with fatal results for all on board. Fortunately for them, it was not necessary to take the navigator and gunners on circuits, only the engineer and wireless operator, so the loss of life was not as bad as it might have been. But I was very upset by the sheer carelessness of it all. It is all very well being killed by enemy action but fatal accidents are completely unnecessary.

On another occasion I was officer in charge of the night flying. With nothing much to do, I was sitting in a low chair at the windows while the three pupils of the last detail were doing their three solo circuits. I was dozing at about three o'clock in the morning when I heard the sound of cannon fire and glass breaking. I slid off the chair until I was shielded by the low wall below the windows, and heard the sound of engines passing just over the roof. The WAAF sergeant watchkeeper seized the tannoy microphone and announced 'Air raid alert'. That was the end of it. Apparently, Bomber Command had been operating that night and a German night fighter intruder had managed to sneak in amongst them, found us with our flare path on and used us as a target of opportunity. He fired at a couple of Halifaxes at Lindholme and at our satellite, who were also flying, but missed them both. The only damage he caused was a few broken windows, but he had an opportunity to create chaos.

Return Flights in War and Peace

Strangely enough, nobody else had heard anything at all. Nobody heard the air raid. Everybody slept through it.

It was while I was at Lindholme that I nearly caused a strike that might have had serious consequences. The flight offices were situated in a row on the outside of the hangar, with doors opening on to the tarmac and the perimeter track. I was informed that the offices were being reorganized and that I had to move my flight to another a few doors along. This seemed to be no problem but when I went to look at the new office I found that it had been empty and there was no telephone. A telephone was essential for me to run my flight so it seemed to me that the most obvious thing to do was to move the telephone from my old office.

I got out my little electrical screwdriver, went to my old office, unfastened the phone then took it to the new office and connected it up. As soon as I had done that I picked it up and heard a very surprised operator say 'Who is that?' I told her that it was the new position for A Flight as we had moved from the other office. The position on the operators' board had been unused up to then and she said she would mark it as now being A Flight.

All went well for a few days until the signals officer happened to be in the telephone exchange when I rang through. He immediately noticed that the position that had been unused was now in use. He asked the WAAF operator what it meant and when he heard the reason he went berserk. He rushed round to see me in my office and told me that he was reporting me to the station commander. 'Don't you realize that all telephones are the concern of the Post Office? If the Union found out that you had been doing this you would have had all the telephone workers in the country out on strike for doing their work and stealing their livelihood.' So I was summoned to the group captain's office where the signals officer made his complaint. The groupie asked me

Back at Lindholme

what I thought and I told him that there was a war on and that I had merely thought that I was doing what was necessary to help things along. I think he really agreed with me, and he just made some non-committal remarks and told me to be more careful in future. And that was the end of it.

In January, I got a bit of bad news. I called in to the ops room to see the report on the previous day's operations, which I tried to keep up with, and was very sad to see that the previous night there had been yet another raid on Berlin and that Haydn Goule, my very great friend, had been pilot of one of those missing. A sad loss.

Lindholme was also the scene of one of the most dreadful fatal accidents that I have ever come across.

I was standing one day on the tarmac when I noticed a Lancaster approaching to land with two engines feathered on the port side. This was something that we did not demonstrate unless in an emergency, because it was not possible to go round again on two engines as you were committed to landing. He was rather high and touched down well up the runway. It did not look as if he could stop in time but he swung port on to the grass where he started to slide sideways until he came to a stop with his starboard wing tip a few feet from the double-decker bus waiting on the road by the guardroom. What happened next amazed me. I was thinking to myself 'Phew, that was a close shave', when he started up the two port engines and taxied away. He had done it deliberately.

I made enquiries and discovered that the pilot was a wing commander who worked in an office in the base headquarters, which was situated at Lindholme. He was in the habit of testing the Lancasters that had just finished a major overhaul in order to keep in flying practice, as he had a desk job. He had the strange idea that to make sure the engineers did a good job, he took up those who had worked on it on the test flight, the landing of which he had just done. There were usually about twenty of these. I would have liked to inaugurate some sort of disciplinary action, but as he was a wing commander and I was a squadron leader I did not feel able to do anything about it, something that I have regretted since.

A few days later I was standing on the tarmac when a Spitfire landed and taxied in. When the pilot got out and took off her helmet, it turned out that she was a very attractive blonde lady with hair down to her shoulders. She was in the ATA (Air Transport Auxiliary), and had a mag drop while delivering the Spitfire, so she had landed at Lindholme for repair. It proved impossible to cure the drop immediately so she had to stay the night and was put up in the officers' mess. During the evening she made the acquaintance of the wing commander, and the two of them became friendly. She became a frequent visitor. One day, when she called he was about to test a Lancaster that had just been overhauled and he invited her to go with him and all the airmen.

She agreed, and they took off. Some time later while they were cruising at about 3,000 feet the nose of the aircraft suddenly dropped sharply. The plane dived into the ground, killing everybody on board. I was devastated for all the passengers but not about him as he had killed them all by his carelessness. There was a small warning notice at the side of the autopilot that read 'Do not engage below 5 thousand feet.' When one was flying a plane regularly one would expect the setting of the autopilot to be the same as where it was when you last used it. But one could not rely on that, so care had to be taken to engage it for the first time you used it. There was nothing to indicate what the setting was. During the inspection the unit would have been wound to its limit to check that it moved freely and left in the fully forward position. When it had been engaged in this position the unit would have pushed the column fully forward, causing the fatal dive that followed. Knowing him and his slapdash attitude to flying, I suspect that he was not properly strapped in, so that he would have been thrown up to the top of the cockpit and in no position to take any action. In any case, it took considerable strength to move the controls while the unit was engaged.

Lindholme was in 1 Group so we had an operations room with all the information available to a squadron. In the new year it became apparent that the types of target were altering. Instead of being German towns, they were in France, and poorly defended. The result was that losses plummeted. Everybody was delighted at this but there was a sting in the tail. It was announced that all trips to French targets would only count as a third of a trip towards the total, so the enthusiasm soon evaporated. However, there was an attack on a French target at Mailly-le-Camp where a German Panzer division was billeted and things went sadly wrong. The marker crews had got a bit over confident, and took a very long time to mark the target, thinking there was no risk. They told the main force to orbit till they were ready, which took them about half an hour. Unfortunately, by then the night fighters from Germany had arrived and had a field day. Over twenty Lancasters were shot down.

French targets were swiftly restored to their position as a full trip.

Chapter 14

Second Tour in 625 Squadron

When one had completed a tour one was entitled to six months' rest from operations before one was eligible for a second tour, which was of only twenty trips. Strangely enough, it wasn't very long before one wanted to get back to a squadron when the six months were up, and one waited for the call to come. When it came depended on what the need was and what vacancies were available. In my own case, it was a bare six months. I did my last trip at Wickenby on 10 November 1943 and I was posted to 625 Squadron flying Lancasters as a flight commander on 12 May 1944. It was a six-month spell almost to the day.

When I arrived, I found that one of the flight commanders had gone missing while taking a new crew, so I had been posted to fill the vacancy. I discovered that the CO was Wing Commander Douglas Haig who had been a cadet at Cranwell in the course before me and we knew each other well.

In the middle of my tour at Wickenby all the aircrews had been told to assemble in a large hall at Binbrook, the base headquarters. When we got there we found that we were going to be addressed by Air Chief Marshal Harris – the CO of Bomber Command. After a short speech he asked if anybody had any ideas, as he would like to pick our brains. Nobody came up with much, not even the Australians of 460 Squadron. Anyway, when I left the building I ran into Duggie Haig, who was then a squadron leader and working at No. 1

Second Tour in 625 Squadron

Group Headquarters at Bawtry. When he was promoted and given a squadron, he sent for me when he lost one of his flight commanders.

Because my predecessor had been lost with another crew, I found that, once again, I inherited one. This time two of the crew were officers: the bomb aimer was Pilot Officer Binns, a Canadian, and Pilot Officer Travis was the navigator. The engineer, Sergeant Robotham, was very old, about thirty years, and we thought it was exceedingly good of him to be flying operationally. But he knew his job and we got on very well together. The other three were NCOs: Sergeant Beecroft, the wireless operator, and Sergeants Jaques and Davies the two gunners. As I was now a flight commander I had a lot of extra duties and did not see so much of them as I had with my previous crew, but we got on very well, and all finished our tour together.

One of the characters in my flight was a warrant officer who had been commissioned while doing his training in Canada but had been reduced in rank after getting on the wrong side of the station commander, reputedly by getting his daughter in the family way! He drove an open green Bentley racing car, which was the envy of us all, but where he got the petrol nobody knew.

The day I arrived, ops were on but only for one aircraft for gardening. I went to the briefing, which was in the operations room. The dropping zone was in a much more hazardous place than the one I went to, in the estuary of Kiel harbour. He had to fly over the Baltic at 10,000 feet then drop down to a thousand as he descended into the entrance to the harbour. Very like dropping into the Thames estuary. It looked a bit dangerous but as long as he kept to his intended track he was fairly well away from the defences, and so it turned out, as he came back safely.

Return Flights in War and Peace

We went on a Bullseye around England for four hours on 12 May, just to get the crew and me used to each other, then on the 21st we went to Duisberg in the Ruhr – a typical Ruhr attack by Oboe. We bombed from 22,000 feet in the last wave with no trouble, just like old times!

No. 625 was a two-flight squadron and it was the accepted practice that the two flight commanders did not fly on the same night so that the one could help the CO to get the aircraft away safely in case of snags. When the CO went both of us stayed on the ground.

When ops were put on the two flight commanders went to the CO's office and it was decided who would go that night. We knew the target by then; it could be either an easy or a difficult one. I found it a bit difficult to decide to put myself forward if it was an easy one, or not if it was a difficult one. But the CO usually made the decision. He himself was only expected to fly about once a month.

My next trip, on 24 May, was an easy French one to a gun battery at a place called Le Cupon. Three days later I went to another one at Marville near where the Normandy landings were to take place. Both these trips were only about three hours each.

I had a few days' leave then so that I could get married on 26 May 1944 to Jean, the WAAF officer I had met at the CFS in 1942.

Jean came from Glasgow, which was a long way away from Upavon and Lincolnshire, so I had not had the opportunity to meet any of her family. Now that our wedding had been arranged Jean told me that her mother was getting embarrassed because when her friends asked her what her future son-in-law was like, she had to tell them that she had never met him. It was necessary to do something about it. I mentioned this to Duggie and he soon came up with a possible solution. Each new crew that arrived in the squadron

SECOND TOUR IN 625 SQUADRON

had to do a long six-hour cross-country. This was always done over the Outer Hebrides where there was no enemy activity and Glasgow was on the track to the Outer Hebrites. So, when the next crew did its training cross-country they could drop me off at Renfrew airfield on the outskirts of Glasgow, and I would have six hours to get in to the middle of Glasgow, have a cup of tea with the family, and get back to Renfrew in time to get my lift home. In fact, he said that he would come on the trip as well. And this is what happened. My mother-in-law was happy, which was most important.

Unfortunately, there was another snag when, with the arrival of D-Day, all leave was cancelled. Fortunately, a week's leave was still allowed for WAAFs to get married, which solved half of the problem. Once again, Duggie came to my aid. He pointed out that a forty-eight pass was not leave, so he could grant me one and as a flight commander I could give myself a day off the day before, and knock off early the day before that. I would therefore have three and a half days to get to London, get married, and return to Lincoln to have my honeymoon with my wife, staying in the Mason's Arms in Louth, a few miles away. And so it came to pass and on 5 June Jean returned from her leave to her station, the headquarters of No. 3 Group at Newmarket.

My next trip was on the night of D-Day, 6 June, to Vire, a town close to the fighting in Normandy. We did not fly again until 22 June, when we attacked a target near Rheims where we bombed from 12,000 feet.

By now, there was a new target as the German V-1 flying bombs, nicknamed Doodlebugs, were in use and we bombed two of their launching sites on 24 and 25 June. They were two very easy trips, which we were happy to put under our belts. But the French targets were not all so easy as we discovered on the 30th when we went to a marshalling yard in Vierzon, in mid-France.

Return Flights - In War and Peace

Since the French targets were small, they did not merit the attention of the whole of Bomber Command, so the practice had developed of each target being dealt with by just one group, so that several targets could be attacked on the same night. Each group attack was usually by about 120 aircraft. This created another problem as there were not enough Pathfinders to go round so each group formed its own marking flight for easy targets, while the real Pathfinders did the German ones. The group marking flights had their master bombers as well, but they tended to take a long time to mark the target because they did not have many aircraft to drop illuminating flares. This is what had contributed to the disaster at Mailly-le Camp.

On this night we were the only group to operate because the weather conditions over England were poor, although they were good over France. As our target was considered the most important one we were the only group to go. We were briefed to bomb from 8,000 feet.

We flew in cloud until we reached the French coast, where the weather cleared to a dark, moonless night with no cloud and very good visibility, as forecast. Soon after crossing the French coast I noticed flares in the sky a long way ahead, and wondered what they could be. We were then about half an hour from the target and as we flew on the flares continued to burn ahead until it suddenly dawned on me that they were in fact at the target, and it was the master bombers seeking their aiming points.

'Christ', I thought to myself, 'this is building up to be another Mailly-le-Camp.' Sure enough, as we arrived the master bomber gave the order to orbit. We did an orbit, taking about a minute, and as we straightened up on the TIs the master bomber said to bomb the red TIs, which had just appeared ahead. As he said this there was a burst of tracer just alongside us and a Lancaster burst into flames. 'Christ,' I

Second Tour in 625 Squadron

said to myself again. We dropped our bombs at 8,000 feet and then there was nothing much to do but head for home, so this is what we did. It was pitch black and we were still at 8,000 feet, with planes going down all around us, above, below and beside. There was nothing we could do but keep a good lookout, keep at the full maximum allowed throttle, and hope for the best. I think it was the fastest that a Lancaster piloted by me ever flew! Fortunately, we did not have far to go, the whole trip was only five hours. But we were very glad when we at last gained the cover of the cloud over England.

Some 115 Lancasters attacked Vierzon that night, and fourteen were lost, which is 12 per cent, a larger percentage than was lost on the famous raid on Nuremberg. Not as many were lost as at Mailly-le-Camp as we were only kept to orbit once, not half an hour, so the fighters did not have so long to congregate.

Our next trip, on 14 July, was to Revigny, which was on the southern side of Paris. Other groups were attacking other targets in the same area and there was a chance that the different groups of aircraft might get mixed up. So to keep us well apart from the others we were routed down to Penzance, round over the sea past Brest and then in to France over the Atlantic coast and so to the target. This was obviously going to be a long trip.

When we approached the target area we could see activity and an aircraft going down. The deputy master bomber called up 'The master bomber's had it.' Another plane was then seen to go down and there were no more transmissions so it was obvious that the deputy had had it too. As there were no TIs and no prospect of any either, we had no choice but to take our bombs home, and we were faced with the long flight back over the sea. This created another problem. We could not land with the cookie on board, so it had to be jettisoned. But we were not allowed to jettison bombs in the Western

Approaches because of the risk of hitting Allied shipping. We therefore had to go all the way back over England and out over the North Sea where we were allowed to drop bombs.

By the time we had done this we had been flying for more than nine hours and I was doubtful that we had enough fuel to get home. We were over Norfolk and it was daylight by then so when we saw a drome we landed. There were already a lot of Lancasters there, and we found that we had landed at Mildenhall, a permanent station with brick buildings where the Royal RAF Display had been held before the war for King George VI. We reported to the watch office, and they told us that there was fog over Lincolnshire and we could not go home yet. We should wait in the mess until they let us know it was OK to leave. We spent a few uncomfortable hours in armchairs, the mess was crowded and it was hard to find anywhere comfortable. Then in mid-morning we got the nod that we could go so we went to the plane, which now had been refuelled, and headed off for Kelstern.

On arrival overhead I called up 'H How here' and got the reply 'Please repeat'. I replied again, 'H How here.' They called again 'Is that Squadron Leader Rowland?' I replied, rather irritably, 'Well, it was when we took off,' and we were cleared to land. The landing run took us past the control tower and I was surprised and puzzled to see several people waving to us.

When we got to our dispersal the ground crew were sitting disconsolately on the chocks and when they saw us their jaws dropped and they jumped up very excited. When we switched off and climbed out they told us that we had been reported missing, which was why they were so pleased to see us. What had happened was that all the other Lancasters that had landed at Mildenhall had been from another squadron, and flying control had only recognized us as H How and did not see our squadron markings. We had therefore been

Second Tour in 625 Squadron

notified to the other squadron and not to 625, who, as they had not been told about us, assumed that we were missing. When we arrived back at Kelstern our squadron adjutant was actually on the phone to the WAAF flight officer at 3 Group HQ at Newmarket to notify my wife that she was probably a widow, so he was able to hastily backtrack on the bad news.

When we got back to our billets we found that the Service Police had already impounded our belongings and we had to get them back. There had been a lot of cases in Bomber Command where thieves had stolen valuables from crews who were missing and the order had gone out back in April that the SPs should keep safe the belongings of any crew as soon as there was any chance of them being missing.

One sad piece of news from this trip was that Wing Commander Connelly had been killed. I had instructed him on Halifaxes at Lindholme. He was a wonderful chap, like so many in the RAF. He was an extremely good officer and I had got to know him quite well and my wife and I had gone out to dinner with him and his wife one evening in Gainsborough.

One day in July I was called in to Duggie's office, where he told me that Group had ordered that I was to go to Binbrook and conduct a court of inquiry into a taxiing accident involving two Lancasters of 460 Squadron the previous night, which had resulted in both aircraft being badly damaged. I was to take with me as assistant Squadron Leader Munslow, the senior flying control officer at Kelstern. Duggie then gave me a very good piece of advice. He had worked at Group for some time and knew how things worked there. He said to me, 'Don't try and whitewash things. Two aircraft have been badly damaged. It was a serious accident and it must have been somebody's fault. Just find out who it was and say so. If you whitewash it they will only send it back to be done again and you will get a black mark against you.'

Return Flights in War and Peace

We went over to Binbrook the next morning and started taking statements from those concerned. The accident had happened on return from an operation, and it was still a pitch black night with no illumination except for the runway lights and weak glim lights marking the perimeter track. Flying control could not see what was going on and were exercising control purely by radio messages from the aircraft. The first plane had landed and gone to the end of the runway where he had turned right on to the perimeter track and proceeded along it towards his dispersal. The second plane landed and came to a stop two-thirds of the way along the runway and then turned right on to the grass until he came to the perimeter track where he turned right along it. He finished up in front of the first plane to land. He then stopped to carry out his checks, and the first plane taxied into him. The pilot of the first plane did not see the second plane's action in the dark and so, assuming that he had landed first and therefore had nobody in front of him, was proceeding along the perimeter track at a fast rate. We found nine people guilty of severe negligence: if any one of these nine had taken the correct action the accident would have been prevented.

The first culprit was the pilot of the first plane who should not have assumed that he had a clear path ahead, and should have taken more care in the very dark conditions. He said that planes were not permitted to taxi across the grass. the second culprit was the engineer of the first plane to land who, in the very dark conditions, should have been assisting his pilot to keep a good look ahead. Instead, he had been filling in his engineer's log book, which he should have been doing when he got back to dispersal and switched off.

The third culprit was the bomb aimer of the first plane who should have plugged in his Aldis light and shone it ahead as a headlight, in which the plane ahead would have been visible. The fourth and fifth culprits were the rear gunner and

SECOND TOUR IN 625 SQUADRON

mid upper of the second plane who were not in their turrets but having a fag together in the fuselage. If either had been in their turret they would have seen the first plane coming and could have given their pilot a warning. The sixth person who was at fault was the pilot of the second plane for turning off the runway when he was supposed to carry on to the end.

During night flying there was an airman stationed with a telephone at the side of the far end of the runway whose job was to notify flying control when aircraft cleared the runway. If he had notified them of what had happened action could have been taken. He was the seventh person at fault.

The fact that at briefing the flying control officer on duty that night had not it made absolutely clear whether or not planes were allowed to taxi on the grass showed that he had been negligent in his briefing and he was the eighth person at fault.

Finally, the ninth person responsible was the senior flying control officer who was obviously not running his unit sufficiently efficiently if pilots were confused about the regulations on the drome. As he was a squadron leader, the same rank as Munslow and me, we thought we had gone as far as we could with that argument as the same thing could have been made against the squadron and station commanders – in fact, even higher!

We sent in our report and a few days later we heard that it had been accepted and that Group were very pleased with it!

On 17 July we went to another Flying Bomb site called Sannerville, then on the 20th we bombed a huge concrete fabrication at Vizernes, which was supposed to be another German secret weapon for firing projectiles at England. I don't think we can have done much harm with our bombs, with no incendiaries, and I believe 617 Squadron with their 12,000-pound Tallboys had a go at it later with more success. We took a passenger with us, a Warrant Officer Carras, who was non aircrew and whom I believe just thought he ought to see a bit of action.

Anyway, the trip was so quiet that he decided that he should do a real one and came with us again on the 23rd to Kiel. We were on the first wave and bombed from 17,500 feet. It was just an ordinary Pathfinder raid, but I saw what appeared to be rockets coming up; at least, I could see them coming up all the way from the ground.

We finished July with a failure; we had an engine failure on the way to Stuttgart and came back. It was quite a coincidence as my only other aborted trip was on my first tour, also to Stuttgart, a city I never got to.

After that it was back to the flying bomb sites on 2 August at a place called Les Landes. This was a very interesting trip with a new system that didn't work. The idea was that Lancasters should formate on a Mosquito, which with the aid of Oboe could bomb a site very accurately, and we should drop our bombs as soon we saw him drop his. We would make a rendezvous with the Mosquito on the French coast then get in formation and keep there to the target. We made the rendezvous with the Mosquito but couldn't keep up with him. We were going flat out but couldn't keep in formation so that when he dropped his we were about a hundred yards behind him so we delayed a couple of seconds before we dropped ours, therefore I don't suppose that the results were very good. Anyway, we never used that system again.

On 4 August we did an interesting trip in daylight to a target called Pauillac, which was an oil refinery down near Bordeaux. To get to it we had to go down to Land's End and then go out over the Atlantic past the Brest peninsula, then come in over the French coast at the level of Bordeaux and head in to Pauillac, which was on the Gironde estuary.

In order to avoid radar detection, we had to fly below a thousand feet. This was extremely tiring as it was not possible to use the autopilot at such a low height. On reaching the coast we climbed to 6,000 feet to bomb, then climbed to 15,000 feet and headed straight for home over France. Bombing from only 6,000 feet, we made a good job of it. The weather was very good with no cloud and we had an easy journey home, with no fighters appearing,

I was well in the front of the bomber stream and wished to get home first, which I usually managed to do. I knew from my experience the best way to obtain the maximum airspeed. The maximum permitted continuous revs were 2,650, and the maximum boost was plus six. It paid to fly as high as possible as the air was thinner and made a difference, and 14,000 feet was the highest height at which you could get that boost at those revs. So you got the best speed at those settings at 14,000 feet. I had also found out that it was a mistake to start losing height too soon, because when you did you came in to denser air and spent time at low level flying much more slowly. But a common mistake was to give way to impatience and start losing height too soon. I knew it was much better to maintain height until you were close to base then come down to the base in a fast power dive. It was a bad error to take too much notice of the indicated airspeed as the true airspeed corrected for altitude and temperature was usually much higher.

One of the American pilots was determined to beat me home. As we passed over Reading I saw him coming up behind us and then wave at me as he put his aircraft nose down and headed for home. I kept my height, and the crew all said 'Come on Skip, he's getting ahead.' 'Not for long,' I replied and watched him as he went ahead as he lost height then started to fall back until he was far behind us. Five minutes from Kelstern I put the nose down, making a fast approach and landing first. He landed five minutes later and I shall never forget the amazement on his face when he saw that we had already landed before him after he had passed us half an hour before.

A few weeks later I was ordered to report to the base commander, Air Commodore Wray, at his married quarters at Binbrook. When I arrived his wife met me at the door. 'He's busy at the moment, but he won't be long, wait in the sitting room.' Not long later he entered, with a smile on his face, and said, 'Ah Rowland, just the man I wanted to see.' He went on, 'Last night there was a risk of fog back at base so I ordered all aircraft to land away. They all did except that six aircraft returned here in direct disobedience of my order to land away. I want you to carry out an inquiry into all these six planes. I don't mind who or why, but I want one person on the hook from each plane, and I'm relying on you to find them.'

'Yes, sir,' I replied and set off to carry out his orders. I took statements from all the crews and it was not difficult to find the culprits. Their reasons were that they had urgent reasons to get back, mostly dates with their girlfriends. In the process, I had to examine the navigators' logs, and I was amazed to see how bare some of them were. In one case, so bare that I imagined that he must have followed another aircraft in order to get to the target! Anyway, I handed in my findings to the air commodore, who seemed satisfied when he saw the results. I did not hear any more but I imagine that a good few severe bollockings were handed out. I have always assumed that I was chosen for this task because of the result of the inquiry into the taxiing accident, so it was nice to know that I was in favour in high places.

After Pauillac it was back to Germany for three trips but not before a very easy one on 10 August to bomb a flying bomb site called Oeuf, where I was very happy to drop our eggs. Geddit!

Second Tour in 625 Squadron

On 12 August we went to Brunswick. This was an experiment that didn't work. When the Pathfinder Force (PFF) was formed the Pathfinder planes were the only ones that had H2S, the new type of radar that was able to get returns from the ground below and show them on a screen. This provided a very rough idea of what was below. Water and coastlines showed up very well but built-up areas were not defined very well. However, if you had a good navigator, which Pathfinder crews did, you could tell if there was a town below. With that information the backers up could drop flares by which the markers identified their aiming points and dropped their TIs for the main force to bomb. H2S had a big disadvantage as the screen did not show what was immediately below as the returns were too strong in a circle of about twenty miles flying at 20,000 feet. You therefore had to do a timed run from the edge of it.

By now, all Lancasters had H2S fitted, which the bomb aimer operated. Someone had the idea that we could dispense with the Pathfinders and let each plane bomb using its own H2S. This was tried and turned out to be a complete failure as the attack was very scattered.

Unfortunately, it was a bit later that the German fighters managed to discover the frequency of our H2S transmissions and used them to home on to our bombers. We were then told only to use the H2S for short periods at a time.

We had a week's leave and then on the 26th we went back to Kiel, bombing at 17,000 feet, but didn't see any rockets this time.

Then, three days later, we had a very long raid, to Stettin on the Baltic coast. The route took us clear of defences over Denmark, then past the Swedish coast until we were north of Stettin, then south to the target and back the same way, taking eight and a half hours. The defences were very poor and we bombed from 11,000 feet. It was quite a sight seeing all the lights on Sweden; we were very careful to avoid their airspace as they were reputed to be very offensive to intruders of any nationality.

By September the invasion of Europe was going well and we had complete command of the air in the whole area, so much so that we were beginning to risk Lancasters doing raids in daylight over the continent. On the 3rd we did an easy attack in daylight on a *Luftwaffe* drome in Holland, Gilze-Rijen by name. The whole trip only took three hours and we saw no enemy aircraft and very little flak. We bombed from 12,000 feet and in very good conditions so I don't think they did any flying from there for a few weeks!

The next day we went to the assistance of the British Army who were surrounding Le Havre. We were warned that we must take great care where we dropped our loads as the targets were very close to the British front line.

We had to cross the coast out at Beachy Head and as we flew down over England it was a lovely sunny day. Suddenly, Binns, the bomb aimer, a Canadian, said 'Skip, we're just coming up to Windsor castle, can I take a photo of it to show the folks back home?' 'Yes, as long as you are sure you don't drop our bombs on it.' 'No chance of that,' he said and the picture was duly taken. The raid was a piece of cake; we hardly crossed the French coast and had almost no opposition.

The camera was to take photos of where the bombs were dropped. The first photo was taken when the bombs were released, the third one of the spot where the bombs landed and the second one halfway between the two. When we got home I told Binns to make sure that he told the camera section what he had done, otherwise they might get things muddled up, and thought no more about it. The next day I was horrified to hear that I had been suspended for dropping our bombs in the middle of the British Army!

Second Tour in 625 Squadron

I realized what had happened at once and was soon unsuspended when I explained the situation, which was soon accepted as soon as it was checked out that no bombs had actually been dropped on our troops.

This op had brought my score to the required twenty for my second tour, making a total of forty-eight for the two. As I liked the idea of doing my fifty I volunteered to carry out the extra two, hoping that they would not be too hard. My next one was a daylight raid to another Dutch airfield at Rheine-Salzbergen, which we again gave a good plastering.

My last op, believe it or not, was to Calais, the same place where I made my first operational flight in my Hector in 1940. I was very lucky to finish with such an easy one, having heard of what some people had to do on their last. (Jack Currie had to fly to Berlin, for example.)

As I was nearing the end of my tour, I started thinking about what posting I would get.

Duggie was in the same position as me and one day he told me that he had got a lovely job to go to. Apparently, BOAC were expanding in preparation for the post-war boom in civil flying, and needed pilots. The RAF was the only source of supply and they had agreed to release, on a two-year secondment, people who had done two tours who they considered had done their share of war service. Duggie had applied and had been accepted, and was awaiting his call. I asked if he would put my name forward and he did so, with the result that I was accepted too.

Duggie also surprised me by telling me that he had recommended me for a DSO. This came through a few weeks later. I felt sure that my activities with the Courts of Inquiry had helped the application to be approved in the higher ranks of the Group.

When I had finished my tour I was posted as flight commander and flying instructor to No. 1 LFS (Lancaster

Finishing School) to fill in time until I went to BOAC. Our task here was to take pupils who had just done the conversion to four-engined Halifaxes at Lindholme and convert them to Lancasters by giving them a demonstration of their flying characteristics, followed by three day and three night circuits and landings.

There was to be a party in the officers' mess and I wanted my wife to come. She was at 3 Group Headquarters at Newmarket. I drove down on the day of the party and collected her and her dog Bonnie, a border collie. I could not spare another day off to take her back so I decided to fly her back to Newmarket airfield, which was on the racecourse. I could not use a Lancaster just to fly her down so I decided to do the familiarizing in a straight line on a course to Newmarket, then land, unload her and do the same on the way home.

I got her and the dog waiting in the flight office and got the Lancaster with the engines running outside, then rushed them in where I made them comfortable on the rest bed. I took off and set course for Newmarket and, sure enough, by the time I had demonstrated the flaps, undercarriage, stalling and feathering the engines, we were over Newmarket. We landed and I taxied over to the far side of the field where there was a hedge on the boundary. I parked the Lancaster so that she would not be seen when she got out. She then did so and disappeared into the hedge and made her way back to her billet. I called up the control tower and said 'Training flight, landed to change pilots.' They replied 'Roger' and we took off and flew home, finishing the demonstrations on the way. It goes to show how anything is possible if you put your mind to it.

I was delighted one day to come across my old 12 Squadron Lancaster V Vic W4990 in the hangar, the one I did most of my first tour in. She had been pensioned off after Pete's death as needing too many repairs to be done on the squadron. The squadron was given a newer and better one in exchange.

I was waiting for take-off one day at the end of the runway when I saw a Lancaster flying across the drome, then a Spitfire flew across as well and knocked the tail off it. The Spitfire went into a dive and crashed about a mile away. The Lancaster put its nose down and from where we were it appeared to have crashed in the middle of the camp near the officers' mess and a column of smoke went up as it exploded. I had just spent a lot of time and money doing up my car and it was parked outside the mess. I have to admit that the first thought to pass through my mind was 'My God, I hope my car is OK.'

We took off and when we were higher we saw that it had, in fact, crashed in the camp. It turned out that it had crashed on a hut that was the anti-gas section. The one occupant had just gone for his lunch as it was midday. This was just across the road from the sergeants' mess which, it being midday, contained about 500 sergeants having lunch. There was a WAAF sergeant standing on the steps of the mess who saw it all from a few yards away. She had such a shock she took days to get over it.

When my posting to BOAC came on 1 December I felt rather sad in a way at leaving the RAF after so many happy years. I looked back at my time there with some satisfaction as I felt that I had done my duty well. Apart from my time in squadrons, I was also pleased with my efforts as a flying instructor. A lot of instructors were a little unhappy at their lot. There was a little poem in *Punch* called 'The flying instructor's lament', which started:

> What did you do in the War, Daddy,
> How did you help us to win?
> Circuits and bumps and turns, laddie and how to get out of a spin.

Return Flights in War and Peace

But they were doing a magnificent job. In the First World War pilots were sent to squadrons with about ten hours' solo, but in the Second World War the training of pilots was as good as was given in peacetime, even better in fact as it now included full instrument flying. When one considers the number of trained pilots who were turned out to a very high standard, the enormity of the task is apparent. To get to a Lancaster squadron a pilot spent fifty hours training in elementary types, and then fifty hours on a service type, when the Wings badge was awarded. Then he had eighty hours at an operational unit, followed by twenty hours at an HCU (Heavy Conversion Unit) and twenty hours at an LFS (Lancaster Finishing School). He therefore had over 200 hours, including night flying. He then had further flying at the squadron before he was passed as operational.

Chapter 15

Seconded to BOAC

On 1 December 1944 I was posted to BOAC at their local headquarters in Bristol, a town that I knew well. They operated their aircraft from Whitchurch Aerodrome, which was where I had done nearly all my flying in 1939 before going to Cranwell. It was quite a small field with only one runway of about 1,600 yards. It was quite suitable for operating empty Dakotas but not for passengers. When we went off on service we had to fly down to Hurn near Bournemouth and pick up our passengers there. A private bus ran from the middle of Bristol every hour to take staff to work.

One disadvantage of this posting was that as I was only an acting squadron leader, I had to drop back to flight lieutenant, with a loss of pay. Also, I was a civilian so had to pay my living expenses myself, although when off on service we got a generous allowance, which just about compensated.

There were about twenty people in my course, all experienced ex-operational pilots like myself. The first thing we had to do was to get fitted out with BOAC uniforms, reasonably smart navy blue double-breasted jackets with trousers and caps to match. I remember that one day as we tried on our new uniforms, one of us, Bill Bailey, said 'I feel like a well to do janitor.'

We had gold rank rings on our sleeves; two rings for us as we were to be second officers, similar to a flight lieutenant.

Return Flights in War and Peace

When we got command we became junior captains with two and a half rings. As we would be flying civil aircraft we would have to get 'B' licences with an endorsement for any type of aircraft that we would fly with passengers. This entailed us going through ground lectures on the Dakota aircraft that we would be flying.

The second necessity was to get up to date with all the inoculations that were necessary for foreign travel. We had to have an inoculation certificate and if this was not up to date some countries would not let you in. I had never had any so they put the whole lot in with one syringe. As a result, I was a bit off colour for a few days.

BOAC fitted us up with lodgings. The ones I had were not very satisfactory but a few weeks later I managed to get a furnished one-bedroom flat with a kitchen and bath. Very conveniently, Jean was posted to RAF Filton on the outskirts of Bristol and was able to sleep out, so it was a very satisfactory arrangement.

I did my first flight in a Dakota on 5 December and training proceeded apace. On 6 January I was sent with three others on a beam approach course at RAF Watchfield, which was completed satisfactorily, but I had a few interesting experiences there. Being an RAF unit, we were all wearing uniform. I remember that we had to sleep in a Nissen hut and as the weather was very cold we had to sleep fully dressed with our greatcoats on top as well. At that time the RAF had a huge surplus of newly qualified pilots who had just come back from Canada and for whom they had no immediate use. They were therefore doing a blind approach course to fill in time until a use could be found for them and also to get them used to British weather after the clear skies of Canada. I had heard that there were 3,000 of them hanging around in England. As the end of the war approached, things improved in the operational units and the losses were very few

SECONDED TO BOAC

compared with the old days, and as a result there were no dead men's shoes to step in to. Not so many replacements were needed and with the Empire Training Scheme coming into full flow this surplus had built up.

On the day we arrived, we went in to the very large dining room for tea. There must have been over a hundred newly commissioned pilot officers in there and there was a hum of conversation. Three of us walked in. I think we had ten decorations between the three of us, three DSOs, six DFCs and one DFM. When the pilot officers saw us, the hum of conversation stopped, and many jaws dropped as a large group of Wannabees saw for the first time a group of Dunnits. It was quite embarrassing.

The next day, I was walking through the streets of Watchfield when the most bizarre occurrence of my life happened. A young lady came up to me and said 'Were you by any chance in Bomber Command?' When I nodded, she said to me 'Would you do me a very great favour?' I said, 'Certainly, if it's possible.' She went on, 'My brother is a pilot in the RAF and he has just been posted in to a squadron in Bomber Command. My mother has heard that the losses in Bomber Command are horrendous and she is absolutely convinced that her son is as good as dead. As a result she has gone in to a state of extreme depression and has taken to her bed and cannot be consoled. When I saw you with your decorations it occurred to me that perhaps you had got through your time in Bomber Command successfully and if that is the case would you be willing to come and speak to her and try and cheer her up, being someone who knows about it. I live in a house just up the road.' I was a bit taken aback by this, but as I had time to spare, I agreed to go with her. She led me to a large detached two-storey house in the next street and took me upstairs where she led me to a bedroom where a very sad-looking woman in her fifties was lying in bed. 'I've brought someone to see you Mother,' she said.

I then had a conversation with the old lady. I told her that I had survived a period in Bomber Command, and that things had been rather dangerous in the past but that even then there were quite a few survivors and that things now were a lot easier with the end of the war approaching and the German Air Force almost non-existent. Losses were now very few, and her son would have a very good chance of surviving. I could not, of course, guarantee that he would do so because in the nature of things flying had its risks, but there was not too much to worry about. I was pleased to see that after our little chat she had brightened up quite a bit. The daughter then came back with a tray of refreshments and we all had a nice cup of tea. When I left, the daughter thanked me profusely for coming to see her mother and said that she had been very much cheered up by what I had said. I have often wondered what happened to the son, and whether he survived. I hope he did, for it would have been tragic for the family if he had not, though that was the case with the families of all the millions who lost their lives in the Second World War. It cannot have been very nice for my own parents during my time in the RAF. Fortunately, as a family we were very lucky in that respect, with my brother also coming back from his long spell in Burma.

One evening I went out for a drink and went in to a pub. When I entered, I found that the pub was crowded with American soldiers. There was a large table in the centre of the bar and a bunch of them were playing craps. For those who don't know the game, it is a form of gambling with dice. One player shakes two dice in his hand and then throws them on to a table or whatever is available. Bets are then placed on what numbers are on top of the dice when they come to rest. There is quite a ritual about the whole thing. The man who is

SECONDED TO BOAC

throwing the dice talks to them while he shakes them, using phrases like 'Be good to me baby' and other such remarks that are supposed to influence the dice so that they come to rest showing a combination of numbers that is favourable to him. Some of the results have a name such as 'Snake eyes' for two ones, which always wins, or loses, I am not sure which. Any bystander is free to place a bet for himself against the thrower. I stood watching this for some time and eventually decided to chance a small bet. So when the bets were being placed on one occasion I placed a pound on the pile on the table and said 'Put a pound on for me.' The player shook the dice in his hands and whispered endearments to them and threw them on the table. The dice came to rest. I hadn't the faintest idea whether I had won or lost, but a voice said 'You win' and I was handed back my pound plus another. I haven't the faintest idea why I won. If the voice had said 'You lose', I would been none the wiser. Anyway, as I was winning I decided that it was a good idea not to bet any more so I pocketed my money and made a sharp exit. And that is the sum of my experience of the game of craps.

Chapter 16

Dakotas

The fleet based at Whitchurch was called No. 1 line. It operated a daily service to Cairo, a twice-weekly service to Lagos in Nigeria, West Africa, and a daily service to Lisbon in Portugal. This last one was a very popular one and there was great competition to get on it.

By the end of January I had got my licence and was ready to go on line. To my delight and amazement, I was scheduled to go with Captain Lewis to Lisbon. This was a wonderful place to go to, as having been neutral during the war the place was very prosperous and all sorts of things were available, including tropical fruit like bananas, grapefruit, oranges etc, which had not yet started to appear in England.

We went to Lisbon on 27 January 1945 and on to Gibraltar the next day. Then we had an eight-hour flight at night back to Hurn, to arrive on the 28th. We had, of course, flown to Lisbon with civil markings.

After a few days off, to my surprise I was sent again to Lisbon on 1 February with Captain Salmon. My luck, of course, couldn't last for ever, and my next trip was scheduled to Cairo with Flight Lieutenant Clift. The route to Cairo was first to Istres near Marseilles, then to Castle Benito near Tripoli. Then we went to El Adem near to Tobruk, then on to Almaza outside Cairo. The plane had left Hurn at 10 am the previous day then changed crews at Tripoli. This was called slipping. Crews handed on their plane to the crew that was waiting, and took over the next plane to come along. If the service was a daily one the next plane came the next day, but if it was a three times a week service they had to wait two or three days, depending on the day of the week. The Cairo service was daily so one could get back to England in about a week. After a week off one went again – it was quite a pleasant way of life

This was my first experience of slipping, but not, unfortunately, the last. I soon realized that the most important thing for an airline to do was to keep the aircraft in the air, earning money. Utilising the crews was not important so at the end of a normal day's flying, the plane had to carry on. This was no strain for the aircraft, which was an inanimate object. But in certain circumstances could be a great strain on the crew.

When the crew handed their aircraft on to the next crew they had just finished a long day's work, having probably started at about eight o'clock in the morning, and were just ready for a good night's sleep. This they had and spent the day relaxing. By the evening they were ready for another night's sleep. But this was when they had to start another stint of flying, by the end of which they were absolutely exhausted.

The other system that was operated on the West Africa route was for the aircraft to spend the night and carry on the next morning with the same crew. This was very nice for the crew but not so good for the aircraft flying hours. The West Africa route did not slip the crew because the airports did not have night flying facilities.

The worst case of crew fatigue that I came across was much later when we were doing the West Africa route direct across the Sahara, which we were able to do in the four-engined aircraft that we were flying then, which could fly at higher speeds and for longer hours, about 1,500 miles at 200 miles per hour.

Return Flights in War and Peace

The first leg was fine for the crew, leaving London about nine in the morning, having had to get out of bed much earlier. On landing about nine hours later at Tripoli, you were pretty tired after a very long day. No problem yet. But the next day when you took on the next service it was early evening and you were ready for bed again. Instead, you were faced with a nine-hour flight at night over the Sahara to Kano, where you arrived in time for breakfast. After a two-hour stop it was a four-hour leg to Lagos for lunch then an hour and a half to Accra. By the time you landed, cleared customs, did the paperwork and had a forty-five minute drive to the Achimota rest house just outside the town, it was about four o'clock in the afternoon. How I managed to stay awake on the last leg to Accra I do not know. I remember that on one occasion when I arrived I was so tired that I collapsed on the bed fully dressed and fell asleep at once. The next thing I remember was being woken by the boy saying 'Eight o'clock massa, cup of tea and time for breakfast.'

I was still fully dressed in bush jacket and shorts and had slept solidly for about fifteen hours.

We arrived at Almaza about dawn and I often experienced a strange phenomenon, the sun coming up twice on the same day. About half an hour before arrival at Almaza, the sun came up. We were flying at 10,000 feet, the highest we could fly without oxygen. As we lost height the sun dropped down below the horizon, then just as we had landed and switched off the sun rose again at ground level!

As France was still classed as a war zone we could not fly in civil livery as we had to Lisbon, so our Dakotas had RAF markings and we flew in RAF uniform. I had been surprised to discover how few aircraft BOAC had, after the hundreds that the RAF had. The answer, of course, was that the BOAC planes spent most of their time in the air. The planes on the Cairo run averaged seventeen hours a day in the air, while the RAF wanted a lot in the air at the same time but they could stand idle for days. We had left Hurn on 9 February and got back on the 17th. We were able to take quite a bit of rationed food home with us, which was a great help at home.

I left home again on 23 February for Cairo but after that I went on a very interesting trip. I was detailed for a Special with Squadron Leader Hunt in one of two planes to take the Czechoslovakian government to Tehran on their way back home via Russia.

We went up to Northolt, west of London, intending to leave the following morning. Mr Benes, the Czech prime minister, was travelling in the other plane. We had Jan Mazaryk, the foreign minister, in ours. The next morning our plane had a snag and it was decided that the first one would go and we would follow the next day. It was very hazy at Northolt, with visibility about 300 yards. We stood on the tarmac and watched the first Dakota taxi out and disappear in the haze. There was a Spitfire from a Czech squadron circling overhead waiting to escort it to the coast. We heard the sound of Dakota engines running up and then the sound of a Dakota taking off. The Spitfire swooped down and left. We all started to move to our transport when a Dakota appeared out of the gloom. It was our other one, which had had a mag drop and had come back for repair. The Dakota that had taken off was an RAF one whose pilot probably wondered why he was having a Spitfire escort to wherever he was going. In the end, it was decided that because of the delay both planes would leave the next day, so we all had a night in London. We did not slip so we spent the night in Castle Benito and also a day and night in Cairo.

The next part of the trip was the exciting part. We left Cairo at dawn and after a five-hour trip landed in Baghdad. We lunched there then it was a short two and a half hour trip over very mountainous country to Tehran. We spent the night there and I had a very interesting walk around the town, where I was able to buy a beautiful Persian carpet for £20.

As we were a Special we did not have to slip on the way home so we made a quick journey back and arrived on 18 March.

After a week off it was back to the Cairo run with Captain Dupee. But then, to my surprise, I was given another Lisbon–Gib trip with a Pole, Captain Wyziekerski. After that, it was back to Cairo for two more trips, finishing on 12 May.

Then, to my astonishment, I was sent on a command course, which I began at Whitchurch on 24 May. I was extremely delighted as it gave me the impression that I was giving satisfaction. The command course consisted of flights to varying destinations around England and another one to Lisbon. Lucky me. After a bit more instruction on the beam approach and a few night circuits at Lulsgate Bottom, which later became Bristol Airport, I was ready to do a few services as captain under supervision.

The first service was very pleasant. On 29 June we flew from Croydon to Gothenburg in Sweden. The second leg that afternoon was to Stockholm and I was looking forward to a good evening out on the town. Alas, it was not to be. We were told that we had to fly to Helsinki in Finland and back. This service was operated on an ad hoc basis whenever enough passengers were available. By the time we got back to Stockholm, it was about 9.00 pm and we only had time for a meal at one of the few restaurants still open. Very disappointing!

The flights to and from Helsinki were only an hour and a half each way, but an interesting experience. We flew at 10,000 feet north along the Swedish coast until we were at a level latitude to Helsinki. Then we flew west to our destination across the Baltic. But I have never seen so many fir trees in my life. They occupied every square inch of the ground below, millions and millions of them. It was a disappointment to see nothing of Helsinki but the airport.

My next supervised trip, with Captain Price-Stevens, took me to new territory, Lagos in Nigeria, and a new type of weather. This was into the tropics where the high temperatures produce incredibly heavy rain.

The first stop was Lisbon. As the service was only three times a week we did not slip but carried on in the same plane, flying on the same day. This was very gentlemanly and a big improvement for the crew. We only stopped for lunch in Lisbon then on that afternoon went for a two and a half flight to Rabat, capital of Morocco, where we spent the night.

We had a long day the next day so we left early for the seven-hour trip to Port Etienne. This was a most boring flight as we flew down the African coast past the end of the Atlas Mountains, clearly visible to port. Port Etienne was just a refuelling stop with nothing there but the airfield and very hot. But the staff there seemed to like it. It was very dry and sandy, completely different to our next stop, three and a half hours later, at Bathurst, capital of Gambia.

Gambia was all jungle with mangrove plants along the river banks, and crocodiles no doubt. The climate there was very hot and humid with crickets calling all the time.

Next day, it was a three-hour flight to Freetown, another hot and steamy place. By now we had changed into our tropical kit, bush jacket and shorts with long stockings.

While staying in the rest house in Bathurst, we met some pilots from BSAA (British South American Airways), the new airline with routes to South America that had just been founded by DCT Bennett, the experienced Imperial Airways pilot who had been the chief of the Pathfinders. Like all of us, they were suffering from the lack of British-built civil aircraft and were making do with converted Lancasters, which were only able to carry six passengers, and those in very cramped conditions. From Bathurst they flew across the south Atlantic to Brazil, a long trip through the intertropical front with severe weather.

Later, when the Avro Tudor was produced BSAA was the first airline to operate them. Unfortunately, two of them, the *Star Lion* and the *Star Tiger*, disappeared without trace in mid-Atlantic. That put an end to the Avro Tudor, although a few were used on the Berlin Airlift, when every available plane was needed. BSAA shortly afterwards folded, having no suitable aircraft.

The next day, we flew on to Takoradi on the Gold Coast, a five and a half hour trip flying at 1,500 feet to stay under the cloud and going through some incredibly heavy rain. I almost expected to see some fish on the windscreen – the water was almost solid.

After another night stop in the BOAC rest house with mosquito netting around all the quarters, and mosquito nets on the beds as well if you wanted them, it was off to Accra, the capital of the Gold Coast, which was only an hour's flight. It was then another hour to Lagos, the capital of Nigeria, our final destination.

As it was only a twice-weekly service, we had four days in Lagos, which were mainly spent on the beach, though we were warned to be very careful about sunburn as it could affect you badly even when it was cloudy. We set off for home and arrived safely four days later on 22 July.

I cannot say that I was very much in love with that trip. I didn't like West Africa at all, neither the climate nor the flying conditions. Malaria was a problem and we had to take Mepacrine daily to combat it, and that tended to make your complexion a bit yellow. It was said that the Gold Coast was so unhealthy that no governor had ever come back to England alive in two hundred years.

Dakotas

This had been a long trip, eleven days, so I had ten days off before my next supervisory trip with Captain Gibson who was reputed to be a bit of a martinet and a stickler for detail. This time was my first visit to India. We left on 1 August, and as the war was now over all the restrictions on our routes had been lifted so we did not have to go to Tripoli on the way to Cairo, but were able to go by Malta, which reduced the distance considerably. The airport in Malta was Luqa. We spent the night there and it was hellishly hot. I spent a miserable night in a sweltering Nissen hut with no ventilation. Then it was on to El Adem and Cairo.

The next day was a very long one. It was five hours to Baghdad then five and a half hours down the Persian Gulf to Sharjah. It was the hottest place I had ever been to then, though I met worse later. We were given soft drinks that were quite salty to keep our levels of salt up to scratch. Then it was another five hours to Karachi where we arrived two hours after dark. This was before the partition of India, when Karachi became part of Pakistan. We had a day's rest then a night flight back to Sharjah and on to England on the 8th. It was quite a quick trip really, considering how far we had been.

This was the end of my supervisory trips, and on 12 September I set off with passengers and crew on my first service as a captain, with two and a half stripes on my BOAC uniform. However, I was still a flight lieutenant in the RAF and so did not get an increase in pay.

From then on for the next few months I was regularly on the Cairo run. It was very pleasant really, though the weather in the Mediterranean in winter could be quite nasty. But we were expected to get through unless conditions were absolutely impossible. We got struck by lightning a couple of times. It was very different to my time in the RAF where we normally only flew in good weather.

The main trouble was the thunderstorms. In daylight, there was not much warning of running into one unless they were isolated and not embedded in other cloud. But at night it was different. When an object is electrically charged and surrounded by differently charged matter, the object will discharge to it. But the discharge will occur from the parts of the body where the curvature of the surface is the highest, that is to say the sharpest pieces. On an aircraft the sharpest pieces were the tips of the propellers and a phenomenon called Saint Elmo's fire occurred when the discharge became so intense that it became visible as a shower of electrical sparks. This phenomenon had been seen on board ships near thunderstorms and the discharge became visible on the masts and rigging and those parts that were sharpest. This was not visible very easily in daylight but at night was very easily seen. When an aircraft was in the vicinity of a thunderstorm it became charged, and the nearer it got the greater it became.

The first sign that you were nearing a thunderstorm was when the tips of the airscrews became visible in rings of white sparks. As you got deeper into the storm the charge increased, the sparks on the props became worse and it could get to a state where the whole plane became enclosed in the St Elmo's fire. This was disturbing and was often followed by being struck by lightning and extreme turbulence. This could get so bad that it was necessary to carry out the standard action of reducing speed, lowering the undercarriage and putting on a bit of flap. Otherwise, there was the danger of structural failure. But if the aircraft did not penetrate further into the storm, the St Elmo's fire on the props faded away and one could relax. I found it very wearing during a long spell of bad weather at night when the sparks appeared several times on the props before fading away after a few seconds because we had missed the thunderstorm again. Very wearing and all for nothing! I always think of it as being like sailing a ship at full speed through a pack of icebergs where the chances of hitting one was fairly low but catastrophic if you did hit one.

I remember once, between Malta and the African coast we were struck by lightning and I went back to the cabin to see how the passengers were getting on. They were nearly all fast asleep and had not noticed anything. But one gentleman was awake and asked me, 'Captain, what were all those pretty lights just now?' 'Nothing to worry about just a bit of static,' I said.

On one occasion, Luqa was not usable so we had to come back by Catania in Sicily, at the bottom of Mount Etna. One day in December we lost the oil pressure in one engine halfway between Malta and the African coast, so we had to feather the engine and land at Benina outside Benghazi. When the engine was checked it was found that the oil drain plug had come loose and dropped out so all that was necessary was to put it back in, fill up with oil and start up. This was a nice surprise, as I had been expecting a long delay. As it was, we were only a few hours' late arriving at Almaza.

Once, when I arrived at the airport at Almaza on the way home, I enquired as usual how many passengers there were to be. To my surprise I was told there were none: it was all freight. When I asked 'What sort of freight?' I was told 'Gold' and there was a lot of paperwork. I had to sign for it and promise not to let it out of my hands until I could get the next holder to sign for it. I went out to the aircraft and climbed on board, expecting to see the passenger cabin full of large packing cases. But to my astonishment the cabin appeared to be empty. 'Where is the gold?' I thought to myself. When I walked up the passage to the cockpit I saw that there was a small wooden box about the size of a shoe box sitting on each seat. The penny dropped. Gold is the second most heavy metal after lead, only very little below it in weight. If anybody ever steals some gold, don't take too much if you are going to carry it away or you won't get very far.

On another service home I had a rather strange occurrence. We had landed to refuel at El Adem, the first stop on the way home, and the nearest airfield to Tobruk in Cyrenaica.

I was sitting in the restaurant with my first officer having a cup of coffee, looking out of the window at my plane being refuelled. An RAF Halifax landed and taxied in and parked itself tail to tail with my Dakota. The pilot then proceeded to run up his engines and the next thing that we saw was the elevators of the Dakota flying through the air, unfortunately not accompanied by the fuselage! I turned to the second officer and said 'You did put the elevator locks on, didn't you?' He said that he was certain that he had, it was his responsibility to do so. We went out to the plane and discovered that he had, in fact, put the locks on but the strength of the slipstream from the Halifax was so strong that it had broken the elevators and the locks as well. There was an inquiry later and I was exonerated fully; all the blame had been put on the pilot of the Halifax. It was lucky that our locks had been put on or I would have been in deep excrement!

The Dakota was a very well designed aircraft in almost every way but this system of locking the controls was absolutely ridiculous. In a Lancaster the flying control surfaces were locked by a mechanism that contained a metal bar painted red, which went across the pilot's seat so that it was impossible for the pilot to even get into his seat while the lock was in place. And something similar was common in many other types of aircraft. The method used on the Dakota was to have tragic consequences in January 1947 when the singer and actress Grace Moore was killed when flying from Copenhagen to Stockholm when the KLM Dakota crashed on take-off because the elevator locks had not been removed. The plane stalled at 150 feet and exploded, killing all on board.

Dakotas

The strange thing was that the pilot was one of the most experienced of the airline.

The Dakota was the military version of the DC-3, which had been flown by KLM for many years, having been preceded by the DC-2, of which it was a larger and more up to date version. KLM had been able to fly its fleet to England when Hitler invaded Holland in 1940. There had been an air race from England to Australia in 1934 and KLM entered one of their DC-2s, much to many people's astonishment in view of the high quality of the other contestants, which included the specially built de Havilland DH88 Comet that won the race. But the DC-2 entered by KLM came in second because, although it flew at only at half the speed of the Comet, it had a very long range with the additional tanks fitted in the fuselage, so that while the Comet with its short range was making its frequent refuelling stops, the DC-2 caught up.

So the Dutch airlines had been flying the Douglas airliners for a long time and the fatal error made by the KLM pilot is very hard to understand.

We had a couple of days' delay while new elevators were obtained and fitted but we made good use of it by paying a visit to Tobruk, which was only about six miles away. There was not much to see there but ruined buildings and a ruined harbour. There was very little activity as the place was of no great civil importance, its notoriety was entirely due to the wartime activities there. There was still a small British Army presence there and as a result there was a NAAFI store. I went in for a look round as in those days of shortages back home one was always on the look out for something that one could not get at home. I was lucky to find a seven-pound tin of corned beef, which I bought and took home to be greeted with cries of delight as we were about to take a holiday in Scotland on a farm near Pitlochry with Jean's family.

The farmer used to rent out his farmhouse while he and his wife and family moved out into the barn for the summer. My mother-in-law had moved up there during the war to get away from the bombing in Glasgow, and the system had proved so successful, particularly for the farmer, that the practice was being carried on in peacetime. But, unfortunately, when the tin of bully beef was opened the contents were rotten. I suspect that the time in the heat in Tobruk was the cause of this as that is the only case I have come across where the contents of a tin had gone off. Not one of my best investments as Tobruk was a long way back to claim a refund!

One advantage of being on the route to Cairo was the shopping, particularly the food that we were able to bring home as it was severely rationed at home. This sometimes caused a bit of trouble with the Egyptian customs as we went through them on the way home. If you took too much they would complain that you were stealing too much of the food of Egypt. One day, I had a chance to get a few Brownie points with the customs, which I thought might be a good thing. I was approached by one of the customs officers to ask if I could do him a small favour. He said that his brother was a medical student and needed a particular textbook on gynaecology but could not obtain it. He had heard that it was readily obtainable in England in a second hand bookshop in London, and he asked if I would be coming back to Cairo again soon. If so, could I do him the great favour of getting it for him? I replied that I was on the regular Cairo run and would be only too glad to get the book for him. He gave me a piece of paper with his name, Mahmoud Eff, and said if I was not about when I came back, to ask and he would be fetched.

When back in London I went to the bookshop, Foyles I believe, and was able to obtain the textbook for £5, quite a sum in those days. But it was a very large volume and I obtained a lot of enjoyment from it myself as it was all about the female anatomy.

When I arrived in Cairo the following week, I entered customs carrying the book. I could not see the man I wanted so I asked one of the others if Mr Eff was about. To my horror, he replied that he had never heard of him, and, making enquiries of the others, they all said the same thing. I was beginning to get worried that I was going to get landed with a large book that I did not want. So I told them that he must be there and showed them the piece of paper he had given me. He looked at it and said 'Ah, Mahmoud.' He shouted out 'Mahmoud' and the man I wanted appeared from a back room straight away. He was delighted with the book and very grateful. Apparently, Mahmoud was his surname and Eff was short for the word *Effendi* which is the Egyptian equivalent for Mr, so he was Mr Mahmoud and not Mr Eff.

There was a good bit of smuggling going on among some crews. Unlike the RAF, where we flew with the same crew members as much as possible, the aircrews in BOAC did not form as regular crews, so on each service you nearly always found yourself flying with three strangers. It was funny seeing the confirmed smugglers testing the other members to find out if they were happy to let them carry on their work. There was a panel in the floor of the Dakota that was easily taken up, and there was quite a large cavity below in which contraband could be hidden. When we landed back in England, we went through customs at Hurn. We had to take all our luggage off the aircraft for this to be done and when the aircraft was empty the customs went over it with a fine-tooth comb to make sure that there was no contraband hidden anywhere. But it so happened that the lever that lowered the undercarriage came down when the wheels were down on top of this panel and was hooked on to it. The result was that this panel could not be taken up while the plane was on the ground. Goods could therefore be put under it and then on the flight up to Whitchurch the panel in the floor could be lifted and whatever was hidden could be recovered. I heard of one pilot who made himself a nice income from bringing back a dozen bottles of Egyptian Cherry brandy, which he bought for two pounds and sold for five pounds to pubs in Bristol. In fact, they were happy to get it because in those days of shortage everybody was on the lookout for extra supplies of everything. This little racket came to an end when we moved to London Airport because crews no longer got back into the plane to fly on to somewhere else, therefore losing the opportunity to recover any loot. And that is the situation to this day. But for those involved, it was good while it lasted.

Chapter 17

Crossing Africa

BOAC was opening a new route, an extension of the Lagos route. The new route was the one across Africa, from West Africa to Khartoum then to Egypt that had been used during the war for ferrying aircraft from America to the Middle East. This route went from Lagos to Kano in North East Nigeria, then due west to Maiduguri, El Fasher, El Geneina, to Khartoum, then north up the Nile to Cairo.

Captain Mayger had done this route before and he was now taking me to learn the route, after which I would be doing it myself. The whole trip there and back lasted three weeks, which was not particularly popular.

We set off flying alternate legs as we were both captains. When we got to Freetown we were not able to land as the runway had been washed away so we had to land at Lunghi, which was the other side of the river and necessitated a long, uncomfortable ride in a lorry.

We night stopped there, then went on to Lagos as usual. Then we set off to the north to Kano, which was in the very dry sub-Saharan belt. From there it was due east into the very hot dry area to night stop in Maiduguri. This was a real dump, just a rest house and a village and a leper colony stuck in the middle of the desert. The insects that came out at night were unbelievable. Thank god that they were all on the outside of the wire screen that surrounded the house.

Return Flights in War and Peace

Next morning, it was off over the desert, past Lake Chad to a stop for lunch and fuel at El Geneina, then three hours to El Fasher and three more to Khartoum. It was very bumpy over the desert, with heat haze up to 10,000 feet, with clear air and good visibility above that.

Khartoum was, and still is, the hottest place I have ever been to. After we landed, when we opened the doors and got out it was like stepping into a hot oven. We stayed in the Grand Hotel, which was a huge improvement on the BOAC rest houses that we had been staying in. It was very comfortable and up to four star standard. I remember that in my room when I felt the bed the sheets were hot to the touch! But one thing that was marvellous was the iced coffee, available on demand.

Next morning, it was north for Cairo, following the Nile. In fact, we did not follow it closely. The Nile travels in great sweeps hundreds of miles across, so when we headed north the Nile headed to port and disappeared from sight, then reappeared an hour later and crossed below us, then disappeared in the opposite direction. It then reappeared in time for us to land at Wadi Halfa after a flight of three hours. Then after lunch it was two hours to Luxor and two more to Almaza.

We had four days in Cairo as the service was to be only twice weekly. But life in a good hotel was pretty enjoyable and I managed to see many interesting things during my stops there, including the pyramids and the Tutankhamen museum. I was able to climb to the top of the largest pyramid, which is forbidden now on account of the large number of tourists who go there. They would soon wear it away if they were all allowed up. The pyramid is made of blocks of stone over three feet high so to climb it was quite an effort. There were plenty of guides waiting to take you up, showing you the easiest path, for a fee of course, but I made my own way, much to their disgust. The top was a flat square about the size of half a tennis court so there was no risk of falling off while you had a look round.

We were also made honorary members of the Gezireh club, which was on an island in the middle of the Nile. It was a country club with a swimming pool and a golf course. A stop in Cairo was no hardship, better than at home really, and certainly vastly better than Lagos or Accra. In fact, it was a great deal better than life in England at that time when England was suffering its post-war blues.

The trip home was uneventful and we celebrated our return in Lisbon with a good night out, when in a fit of exuberance Mayger and I each bought a large bottle of brandy, four-bottle size. When we saw them the next day we were a bit shattered and wondered how we would get them through customs in England as the usual allowance free of duty was one bottle. However, when we got back we managed it by hiding them under the floorboards.

After that, I found myself regularly on this run but cannot say that I was very pleased to be on it. For a start, the trip was three weeks away and only about ten days at home, which as a newly married man I was not too happy about. By this time I had had to leave my rented one-room flat because the landlord's son had come back from the war and they wanted it for him. In those days you could regain possession of rented accommodation if you wanted it, with due notice of course. We were in a bit of fix as we could not get anywhere else to go. The only thing the estate agents had available was a large house at Westbury on Trym, on the outskirts of Bristol. But the rent was ten guineas a week, which we could not afford. However, I had a stroke of luck when I ran in to Bob Noden who had been in Bomber Command with me; it was he who had given me my dual on the Lancaster at Lindholme. He was in the same position as me so we agreed to share the house together, which brought my share of the rent down to an acceptable level. His wife Jean had been the intelligence officer at Wickenby so I knew her well. There was also the advantage that when Bob and I were away on service the girls had company together and were not left alone. The house had six bedrooms so there was no problem there and we were also able to put up friends as well.

This lasted well until 1946 when the new London Airport opened, on the site of an old airfield called Heathrow. A big, new runway was built that was large enough to take the largest aircraft in use at that time. I remember coming back to London on the day that it opened. There was nothing there but the one runway and a few temporary buildings. One memory is that the customs shed was a marquee and it was all on the side of the great West Road as it was called in those days, before anybody had thought about motorways. It is hard to believe what it was like in those early days when you look at the vast construction that exists today.

One way in which the building of London Airport affected us was that BOAC split up in two, the new branch being called British European Airways. This was to be based at London Airport and the crews who were transferred to British European Airways were the ones who had accommodation in or near London. I was not one of those, but Bob Noden was and he became one of the founder members of the new airline.

This left me with all the rent to pay myself, which was going to be difficult, but as they say, when one door shuts, another one opens. My landlord was a meteorological officer in the RAF and he was demobbed. He was a member of the Wills family, the big cigarette and tobacco company. They were the main competitors of the Players Company in the cigarette market and sold the Woodbine brand, which was very popular. They also owned two huge red-brick Bonded

Tobacco Stores, which were a landmark down in the dock area, so he was not short of money. He was not married and did not want to live alone in a big house, which he would have had to do if he gave us notice to leave. So we came to an agreement with him that we would stay there rent free with him as a paying guest.

This worked very well until the time came when we had to go up to London ourselves. This happened in 1947, by which time I had retired from the RAF and had been given a contract by BOAC as a junior captain at a salary of £1,200 per year, with annual increments of £50 per year. This necessitated my moving up to London and I lived with my brother David in his flat in Kilburn. We were looking for a house to buy but found it very hard to raise the money. It was quite easy to get a mortgage but the deposit that we had to pay was always just out of our reach. The cheapest houses at that time were about £3,000 but anything really good was around £4,000. It seems ridiculously cheap by present standards, but it seemed dear at the time. We toured the western suburbs of London at every spare moment while I was at home. Then one day in 1947 I arrived home from West Africa to be greeted by my wife with the words 'I've bought a house.' I felt a bit doubtful at first but it turned out to be a very good buy. It was a detached bungalow in Ruislip for which the North West Building Society gave us a mortgage of £2,150 on a purchase price of £2,750 so we only had to put down £600, which was well within our means on my salary, with monthly payments of £13- three shillings and five pence per month. I called back there a few years ago and was told that on today's market it would fetch about £185,000. If only I still owned it! We had very little furniture, only a bedroom suite with twin beds, and I helped things along by bringing various pieces of furniture back with me from Accra. The bungalow was also well positioned, being close to London Airport. We were flying from there now and Whitchirch was abandoned,

I was now regularly on the horseshoe route to Cairo via West Africa. The long leg to Cairo was not without incident. We usually took on different passengers for the leg from Accra to Cairo. One day, we had nineteen passengers, a Mr Farhit, Mrs Farhit and sixteen little Farhits aged one, two three and so on up to sixteen. There was also one middle-aged English lady travelling by herself. Mr Farhit was a Lebanese gentleman who was taking the family home for a holiday in Beirut. Mr Farhit was obviously not short of money. He had done very well for himself in Accra. It was said that the Lebanese were very successful because they had the brains of an European but were prepared to live like a native, unlike the white Europeans who had to live at a much more comfortable level, which of course cost money.

We set off early in the morning and arrived at Kano midday where we stopped for lunch. I noticed that all the Farhits had a very good lunch, all eating as if they had not had a good meal for weeks. I was slightly concerned as I knew that it would be very bumpy in the afternoon when the heat of the day caused bad upcurrents off the desert. After lunch we set off for Maiduguri and sure enough the bumps were quite severe so after about an hour I decided to take a look and see how things were in the cabin.

When I opened the door the smell was frightful and I saw that everybody except the English lady was being sick. The lady looked very uncomfortable, which was not surprising. I went up to her and said 'Would you like to come up to the cockpit for a breath of fresh air?' She nodded and followed me forward. I put her in the first officer's seat and opened her sliding window, which I could do in a Dakota as it was not pressurized. This created a nice draught and she soon recovered, and I asked her where she was going to. 'To

Maiduguri,' she replied. This surprised me, so I said 'What on earth do you do there?' She replied, 'I am the doctor in charge of the leper colony in Maiduguri.' As I cringed and pressed myself closely to my left and as far away from her as possible, she laughed. 'Don't worry, leprosy is not nearly so contagious as people think. The general belief is that you have only to touch a leper and you have caught it yourself, but that is nonsense. If you live with a leper, your whole family and all the pigs, the goats, the chickens and all the livestock in a one-room mud hut that never gets cleaned out, after about two years you might catch it. But you are quite safe here with me.' So I was able to relax, very relieved.

On another occasion we arrived at El Fasher to find that we were taking on an extra passenger. He was the local sheik and I think he was not too happy about having to fly. He had to get to Khartoum in a hurry and his family had persuaded him that by air was the best way but he obviously did not have too much faith in his safe arrival, as he had a long string of beads in his lap and he did not stop telling them from the time I saw him until he arrived in Khartoum. There was a habit with some wealthy sheiks in the Middle East of presenting the pilot with a nice gold watch in thanks for a safe journey, but I am afraid to say that this did not happen in my case. Perhaps the journey was too short.

It was while I was on the West Africa run that I saw something that I am sure very few people on earth have seen. After this, I knew that there was no pot of gold at the end of a rainbow because a rainbow has no end. Where the ends should be they are hidden. I was on the leg from Freetown to Takoradi, flying about mid-morning past a large thunderstorm with heavy rain falling from it. I looked across and saw a rainbow, but to my astonishment I saw that the rainbow formed a complete circle. It was such a beautiful sight that I went back in to the passenger cabin and told the passengers who all crowded to the windows on the starboard side to see this phenomenon, to everyone's amazement.

I had a bit of trouble with a wisdom tooth that had been so difficult to extract that the dentist had had to use brute force to get it out, and in the process a bit of my jawbone had been broken off. I had thought that this trouble was over. One day, while on the leg to Khartoum, I found I was getting pain in my mouth where something was cutting in to the side of my tongue. When I arrived in Khartoum I said to the agent 'I need a dentist. Is there one in Khartoum.?' 'No problem,' he replied, and took me in to the town to a dentist's office. I was a bit doubtful about what would be available in such a backwoods part of the world, and had visions of all sorts of unspeakable things being done to me by some unqualified practitioner. But I need not have had any misgivings about it. I was shown into a beautifully clean and equipped room where a charming English-speaking man asked me to open my mouth. With a small pair of tweezers he extracted a small, sharp piece of bone, which was a piece of my jawbone that had broken off and just worked itself to the surface. And that was all.

Chapter 18

Haltons

BOAC was getting a lot of stick then about all the money that they were losing, but it was not really their fault as they had no decent aircraft of any size and the Dakotas were out of date and too small. There were plenty of American planes available, the DC-4 and the Constellation, but they all had to be paid for in dollars. England was nearly bankrupt and the government would not release the dollars necessary except for a few Constellations to use on the North Atlantic. None of the Brabazon planes had materialized so it was decided as a makeshift measure to adapt some of the RAF aircraft. The Lancaster had too small a fuselage to be of any use but the Halifax was more roomy, and a model called the Halton was designed with a cabin for eight passengers and a steward.

A group of pilots went up and collected several Halifaxes, and we started learning to fly them at Aldermaston in order to be ready for the Haltons when they arrived. I was one of those selected and on 25 March 1946 did a short week's course and got them endorsed on my B licence. That done, it was back to the Dakotas on 6 April to fly the horseshoe service until the Haltons arrived.

I had decided to obtain a navigator's licence so had studied and passed the necessary exam to obtain a second class navigator's licence, which I obtained on 18 May 1946.

Spurred on by my success, I burned the midnight oil to study for the first class licence, which I obtained on 3

Return Flights in War and Peace

November 1947. This came through just in time to fly the first Halton from London to West Africa. Passing the exam was rather amusing for me. For a few days before the exam I went to the BOAC navigation school to brush up my preparations. When I turned up on the first day a navigator saw me and said, 'What are you doing here, John?' I told him I was brushing up before taking the first N exam the following week. He roared with laughter and, turning to a group of other navigators who were also taking the exam at the same time, called out to them 'Hey chaps, look at John here. He thinks he can pass the first N exam next week.' And they all fell about laughing.

When the paper for navigation plotting occurred, the problem set was something on the lines of 'You are the navigator of an aircraft that has left Sydney at 0800 hours local time to make an interception with an aircraft carrier which at 0900 hours was in the position Latitude xxx Longitude xxx and steering a course of 260 at 22 knots. Using the chart provided, work out the course your aircraft will have to steer at 225 knots to intercept the carrier, and at what time and position the interception will take place.' It was a fairly standard type of question but to make it a little more difficult the task involved crossing the international date line, so as to complicate the time calculations a very little.

Three hours was allowed to complete this task. I was well in to this when after about an hour one of the navigators got up and went to the invigilator and spoke to him, asking about the local time given in the question. The invigilator studied it for a moment, then said, 'There's a slight mistake in the question paper; when it says local time it should be GMT time. But it doesn't matter just carry on as if it was right.' At that there was a gasp of dismay from nearly everybody but me – pencils were thrown on the floor, papers thrown down and a few people even left. I wondered what all the fuss was

HALTONS

about as in my ignorance I had not found anything wrong. But they had all assumed that it was a trick question and modified their calculations accordingly. They now had to start their plotting again from the beginning but as an hour was wasted they did not have time to finish. Anyway, when the results came out, they had all failed that paper, but I passed. The pass mark was I believe 70 per cent and I got 71.

The services in the Haltons were very different to those in the Dakotas. As they were four-engined they had a much greater range so a lot of the stops could be omitted. The first service I did in them in November 1947 was from London to Casablanca in Morocco. We stayed in the Anfa Hotel, first class, in which Roosevelt and his party had stayed during the Casablanca conference. We slipped, and two days later flew direct to Bathurst where we slipped again. After that, we went direct to Takoradi, missing out Freetown, and on to Accra where we terminated the service and slipped again. We did not carry on to Lagos. This was very acceptable as Accra was a much better place to stay than Lagos and had quite a nice rest house with tennis courts, and also a much better beach that had quite good waves on which you could surf quite well. Not the big boards that you could stand on but shorter ones where you could lie on. We were warned not to go out beyond the surf as there were lots of barracuda there that liked a nice mouthful of human leg.

The flight back to Bathurst was done in daylight as Bathurst Airport had a runway that was pretty crummy at the least, and not suitable for night landings. I did not like this leg at all as the thunderstorms were gigantic and we had one or two nasty moments, so it was a great relief when it was announced that we were to use a new route to West Africa that the Dakotas could not do. This route took us by day from London to Tripoli, where we slipped, then across the Sahara by night to Kano. This enabled us to use the stars for navigation across an area with not much in the way of landmarks, although I did once fly across the Sahara with no difficulty by day, with the benefit of the drift sight. We arrived at Kano at dawn for breakfast then on to lunch at Lagos with finally an hour and a half leg to Accra. By the time you landed, went through customs and got to the rest house and got to bed, it was about half past four.

From the pilots' point of view, the Haltons were OK but for BOAC they were an absolute disaster as they were the same cost to fly as any other four-engined aircraft, but they were only getting eight fares to cover it. They had managed to fit a small passenger cabin in to the fuselage with four seats on either side of the gangway. In front of the passenger cabin there was a small steward's galley behind the cockpit where drinks could be warmed up and simple meals served. Having a steward on board who could keep the crew supplied with hot coffee was a great improvement, although it was not too good for the passengers.

Chapter 19

Yorks

Fortunately, a slight improvement appeared in the form of the Avro York, which was a Lancaster wing with a bigger body. It could carry twenty passengers with a steward and two toilets as well. As soon as these were available we converted to them. I flew these for the next couple of years on the routes to Calcutta and Accra without much trouble except for one day when we took off from Basra, on the way home from India. The starboard outer engine cut the instant that the wheels left the ground. We feathered the prop, and staggered around the circuit, never getting above a hundred feet. We turned port away from the dead engine, which was customary practice, and headed in and out among the palm trees. The strain of turning against the good engines was terrific and by the time we were lined up with the runway I was near the limit of my strength. Anyway, we got down safely. We had a few days waiting for a new engine to be fitted, but that was quite pleasant as Basra was not so dangerous as it is now!

Going to India was a new experience for me after all my time on the West Africa run. Previously, my only visit had been with Captain Gibson on my command supervisory service and then I had only gone as far as Karachi. By now, India had been separated and Karachi was now in Pakistan. There had been huge riots in India during the partition and some of our crews had been in the middle of it. I heard stories from some of those who had been in Calcutta at the time, of looking out of the window of their hotel and seeing mobs on the road outside slaughtering each other by the dozen. The airport at Calcutta was called Dum Dum, and there was an arsenal on the road into the city called Dum Dum, which was where the soft-nosed bullets of that name had been invented. During the partition riots a mob had stormed the arsenal and seized two English supervisors and, despite the efforts of the loyal employees to stop them, had thrown them alive into the furnaces that were going at full blast. I always felt a bit nervous every time we went past the gates on the way from the airport to the city centre.

One thing that puzzled me for a long time was the way that all the small dwellings seemed to have what looked from the crew bus to be oyster shells stuck on the walls. The answer was rather bizarre when I found out. Calcutta was infested by hundreds of cows roaming the streets. This was because cows are sacred in India. Of course, this resulted in the streets being showered with vast amounts of cow manure. Not wishing to let all this manure go to waste, as well as solving the problem of getting the streets cleaned up, the local inhabitants had thought of the ideal solution by turning a problem into a benefit. They scooped up the cowpats in their hands and slapped them against the walls of their houses where they stuck, being of the right constituency. Over a period of time in the hot climate these cowpats dried out until, when they were fully dry, they fell off the walls onto the ground, where they were picked up and stored. For what purpose you may ask. To use as fuel in their cooking stoves was the answer. I wondered if this resulted in the food having a delicious flavour. The dried cowpats, of course, were not needed for heating in those parts.

Calcutta itself was an amazing sight. I had not believed that so many people could live in the same place and with most of them in extreme poverty. The streets looked like the streets of Britain just as a crowd is coming out of a football stadium after a match has finished, plus a liberal sprinkling of cows. There were double-decker buses that in England would have been restricted to all the seats downstairs and upstairs being occupied and no passengers standing, except for possibly a few on the entrance platform. Out in Calcutta, all the seats were occupied, both upstairs and downstairs, both passages were full of standing passengers, and there were two people standing on every step of the stairs. There were ten people sitting on the roof. There were three people sitting with their legs astride the bonnet, and half a dozen on each side, hanging on with one arm. At night, the pavements were fully occupied by half-naked people sleeping; people whose total of wealth was the loincloth that they were wearing. If we went out we had to walk in the middle of the road to get back to the hotel. Having been flying all day, we were hungry and so we were usually the first people to enter the dining room. Labour was obviously cheap in India. There was a waiter for every seat, plus a head in charge of each table. Above them there was a super head waiter for each quarter of the dining room. Finally, there was a *maitre d'hôtel* in charge of the whole lot. All the lowest level of waiters wanted us to sit at their table, and we eventually sat at the table where we were literally pushed to. When we sat down we were hemmed in by a solid block of waiters about three ranks thick. When we went to our rooms late at night we had to go up in the lift because there was a scantily clad servant sleeping on every tread of the staircase.

So all in all, I was not much enamoured with India. The safety of food was also a problem, which was particularly dangerous in Karachi. I know of one pilot who would not eat anything in Karachi except hard boiled eggs!

Fortunately, I was not on the Calcutta run for long before I was put back on the route to West Africa, which was by the same route as we had done in the Haltons across the Sahara desert from Tripoli to Kano. As I was one of the few York pilots who knew the route I was moved over to it.

Although I had missed getting involved in the India rioting, I did not escape trouble altogether as there was trouble in Tripoli also. One day, as I was walking down one of the main streets I saw a mob advancing towards me, waving staves and all sorts of weapons. I heard another noise behind me and then I saw a line of armed police blocking the road. All the other pedestrians seemed to have disappeared and I was left all by myself between the two bands of contesters. On both sides of the street there was a solid line of shops that had metal shutters, which were lifted up when the shops opened and lowered down to ground level when they were closed. Having seen the situation, all the shopkeepers were hauling down their shutters, and I swear that I was able to slide under the last one when it was about six inches from the ground. I was safe there and very soon afterwards I heard a great commotion outside as the two parties commenced battle. The shopkeepers were very helpful and I was able to escape by the back entrance.

When we had been going to Tripoli in the Dakotas we had stayed the night in the ex-Italian barracks at Castle Benito, but now that the war was over we stayed in a hotel in the middle of Tripoli and this was much better. The hotel we stayed at was the Albergo del Mehari, which translates as 'The Camel Hotel'. This was on the seafront overlooking the harbour and there was an underground walkway that led from the hotel entrance under the road to the restaurant on stilts over the harbour. We were allowed a certain amount of money to enable us to dine off the fixed menu, but we were able to pay the excess if we wished to have the *à la carte*. I have many happy memories of dining off a Bismarck steak, which was a steak with a fried egg on top. This does not seem very much in present days but then, when food was very short back home and severe rationing was still in place, it was a real luxury, accentuated by the beautiful surroundings of the restaurant over the water.

Although the water in the harbour looked very picturesque, it was absolutely filthy. There is no tide in the Mediterranean so there was no change of water in the harbour so over the years it had all the filth that had been deposited in it. It was a man-made harbour, consisting of two curved moles that ran out from the shore until they nearly met, leaving a gap of about fifty yards for vessels to pass in and out. It was not possible to swim in the harbour but outside it the water was marvellous, absolutely crystal clear – so clear, in fact, that you could see quite clear to the bottom.

There was a perfect beach on either side of the harbour with lovely clean fine sand. To get to the beach to the west of the harbour, it was necessary to spend a little money hiring a gharry, a small horsedrawn taxi, as it was about two miles away. However, we usually went to the one on the east end, which was only a few hundred yards from the hotel. The only time this was spoiled was one day when an American aircraft carrier came to visit and, being too large to enter the harbour, it anchored just outside. Unfortunately, there was a strong breeze blowing that pushed all the rubbish from the carrier straight to our beach, and one day I was disgusted to find that while doing a crawl I had grasped something disgusting in my hand. So we had to abandon it for the day.

At the other beach we found a new and rather novel method of gambling. There were some beetles walking around on the sand. It was discovered that if you buried them in the sand they would soon find their way to the surface, and however deep you put them before they were buried they soon came to the surface. The result was that we had a lot of fun burying one of these beetles a long way down before covering it over with sand. Drawing a cross in the sand with a finger to form four segments, we would then lay bets on which sector it would appear in.

There was a hospital ship in the harbour that I was able to visit one day when I hired a small dinghy. This was good fun, as was watching the repair work going on to the moles that had been damaged by bombing. I have always found that there is nothing more pleasant than watching somebody working! There was a bunch of businessmen staying in the hotel who were involved in salvage of the damaged ships that were in the harbour. Although they looked like scrap, apparently there was a lot of money to be made out of all the electrical winches that they had on board and which were in very short supply and fetched very high prices

So, all in all, there was plenty to do in Tripoli and I enjoyed my time there very much. It is a great pity that in the present political situation travel there is not welcome. But I am sure it would be a wonderful holiday resort if it were possible. The climate there was always comfortable, never too hot and never too cold, with almost no rain.

I had one rather strange event flying down from Tripoli to Kano, when my navigator let me down. He had not flown this route before so I warned him about a trick of the weather to watch. All the way across the Sahara there was an easterly wind, giving us starboard drift. To counteract this it was necessary to steer ten degrees to port. But about an hour from Kano the wind changed to westerly, which needed a change of course to starboard to counteract it. This was easily discovered by use of the drift sight.

When we were half an hour away from Kano, at 10,000 feet, we started to let down. By now it was broad daylight when we were down to 2,000 feet. Ten minutes from ETA there was no sign of Kano and there was no sign on the radio compass, which by now should have been showing straight ahead. I said to the navigator, 'Did you remember to check the drift?' 'Sorry', he replied, 'I forgot.'

I realized at once what had happened. The wind had changed and we had continued steering ten degrees left while we had ten degrees' port drift, making a total of twenty degrees off course to port. I turned on to a westerly course and climbed up to 10,000 feet again. Ten minutes later the radio compass picked up Kano straight ahead and twenty minutes later we arrived at Kano. We must have been about a hundred miles off track when we turned.

The time was coming up to the end of my two years' secondment. I decided that I liked the life in BOAC so I applied to them for a contract, which they were dishing out now that the war was over. They offered me a contract as a junior captain, so I asked to retire from the RAF and signed up to it. Duggie Haig, my old CO of 625 Squadron, decided to go back to the RAF.

My wife then presented me with a problem. The house that we had bought had been chosen by her, but she was not entirely happy about it. The sitting room was not quite big enough, so she said it would be a good idea to knock a wall down and build another one so as to make the sitting room a bit bigger and make one of the bedrooms a bit smaller. I held out for a bit as I thought it would be a lot of work for not much benefit. However, I gave in eventually, like all good husbands do, but said we should get a builder's advice about the alterations. When he inspected the wall he pronounced that it was a load bearing wall and that if it was taken down it would need a support of some sort such as a steel RSJ. This, of course, was not obtainable as all building supplies were in short supply in those days as everything was needed to build new houses, which were urgently needed. The only answer was to obtain a second-hand wooden beam. These, naturally, were difficult to obtain, so eventually I had a brainwave and said that on my next trip to Accra I would get one there and bring it home.

I was off to Accra soon and when on my slip of two days I set about getting what I wanted. I went down to the BOAC office and told the man in charge what I intended to do and asked if it would be possible for him to let me have some transport out to the airport. 'No problem', he said, 'Let me know when you're ready and I'll let you have a pickup truck.' I then went down to the market and asked about, and was told that there was a sawmill there and they would let me have whatever I wanted. When I got to the sawmill it was not exactly what I expected. They had several large mahogany tree trunks but they were sawing them up by hand. The logs were suspended over a pit about eight feet deep. There was one man seated astride the log and another one standing in the pit and between them they had a huge double-handed saw with which they were sawing planks off the log. This seemed to be very hard work but the finished results were quite satisfactory. I told the boss what I wanted, a four-inch by eight-inch beam about eight feet long, and he took me to a pile of sawn timber and produced exactly what I wanted. The price was very low, about a pound I think, and I told him I wanted to get it out to the airport. He said, 'That's easy, Charlie here will take it out for you,' and he pointed to a well-built man standing nearby. 'How will he do that?' I asked. He replied, 'He'll carry it out on his head. It'll cost you three shillings.' 'That's ridiculous. It's three miles. I'll get a pickup and be back here in no time.' I went back to the BOAC office and saw the man again and true to his promise we headed back to the market in the truck. When we got there, there was no sign of Charlie and the mahogany beam. 'Where is he?' I asked. 'He's gone. He left a few minutes ago.' 'How did you get it on to his head?' I asked. 'We lifted it on for him. 'He's got a pad on his head, he'll be all right.'

I got back in the van thinking that he couldn't have gone far and we would be able to put the beam in the pickup when we saw him. We drove out of the market and along the road to the airport. But there was no sign of Charlie until we were well out of the town. I was beginning to think that we had gone a different way, as he couldn't possibly have gone as far as this, but as we came to the straight leading up to the airport there was Charlie going at a fast lope with the heavy beam on his head balanced with his hands. We came up to him and stopped and told him to put the beam in the pickup. He did not want to do this but I insisted and paid him his three shillings. When we got to the airport we pulled up outside the warehouse. There were two porters waiting there so I asked them to carry the beam in to the store. They got the beam out of the pickup on to the ground then said 'It's too heavy for us to carry in; we'll have to get some help.' When they came back with a third porter they then had difficulty, with much grunting and groaning, in getting it in to the store. Since then, I have never come across any physical feat that equals what Charlie did that day. People do not believe me when I relate this story, and perhaps the reader will also not believe me, but I can swear that every word of the story is true.

In the event, it was all unnecessary as when I was home on my next rest I was able to obtain a second-hand timber beam that fitted the bill perfectly and the job was done to my wife's delight. As the mahogany beam was not needed there was not much point in bringing it home. I was afraid, also, that BOAC might have wanted to make me pay carriage, which might have been very expensive, as the thing weighed a ton and definitely didn't come within the limit for crew baggage. So I never went back to the warehouse to claim it, so maybe it is still there, too heavy for the porter to carry out.

Chapter 20

Grounded

I had a pleasant life for a year then the news came through that BOAC had cracked the dollar problem. They could have DC-4s built in Canada fitted with Rolls-Royce Merlin engines made in England. These were Canadair 4s, called Argonauts, which duly came in to service and did sterling work till better things came along.

I was among those to be selected to convert on to them. But, all of a sudden, I began to wonder if there was any long term future in civil aviation. It seemed to me to be getting nowhere. I never imagined that it would develop into the colossal industry it is today. So when my mother offered me a job in the family hotel business, I gave in my notice and left BOAC. It was the biggest mistake I have ever made in my life and I have regretted it ever since.

And that is the end of the story about my flying career.

I often wonder what would have happened to me if I had stayed with BOAC. The first thing I wonder about is Comets. When I left, the question of jets was just a small cloud on the horizon. I can remember an occasion when the question of jets was being discussed and one of our captains said that it would be very dicey flying them because they were so fast that it would be suicidal to fly into thunderstorms, because we had to do that quite frequently. The standard procedure was to reduce speed as low as possible, lower the undercarriage and put down a little flap so that we could ride the turbulence without the aircraft breaking up. The consensus was that he was right but the only thing to do was to wait and see. In the event, the problem never arrived because jets, when they arrived, cruised at about 40,000 feet, which was way above the tops of the thunderstorms.

When they arrived, it turned out also that the Comets did not carry navigators. Because they were also used on long stages, it is a legal requirement that they should carry a qualified navigator with a first class licence. In addition, there was a change in the pilot's licence. The old B licence was to be scrapped and replaced by the ALTP licence (Air Line Transport Pilot), the holding of which required navigation qualifications. This brought about a huge training of pilots to enable them to get the new licence and carry on their employment. As I already had a first class navigator's licence this would have been no problem to me, and I think I would have been certain to have gone on the Comets.

In view of the three Comets that crashed, I wonder whether I might have been on one of them if I had still been there. In any event, it would have been very unpleasant flying them while they were suspect. Two of those that lost their lives were Captain Haddon, who had been the instructor on my command course on Dakotas, and Captain Gibson, who had taken me under supervision to Karachi.

I realize that I am an extremely lucky man on several counts. First of all, I lived through all the years of the war, while having a flying job all the time, whereas so many others fell by the wayside. I was lucky to be able to live through it all in comfort. I always feel a bit guilty when I read of the tribulations endured by some others. I think of those crews in submarines, people like my brother, David, who fought in the jungle in Burma and those fighting on the eastern front in Russia, whereas I can honestly say I enjoyed every minute of it. And I had experiences that thousands would like to have had. Against this, I lost dozens of very good friends who are sorely missed, as well as hundreds of acquaintances – fine men, who were not as lucky to survive as I was.

After the war, Bomber Command has received rather a bad press, both on the grounds that area bombing should not have been carried out, and also because it was considered, by some, a waste of effort and had no effect on the winning of the war.

Regarding the first, I have often been asked whether I have any conscience about all that I did in Bomber Command and I always answer 'No'. I take the same view as Air Chief Marshal Harris who said 'They sowed the wind and they reaped the whirlwind.' There is no doubt at all who started it, with a history of attacks going back to the destruction of Guernica during the Spanish Civil War. And Hitler on many occasions caused weak countries to capitulate by threatening them with the destruction of their cities by his mighty *Luftwaffe*. I am proud to have been an officer in the first air force to take them on and beat them. During the war, I was often asked by civilians about what I was flying, and when I said I was flying bombers to Germany the reply that I got was always, 'Good show, give the bastards hell.' It is only after the war that criticism has begun.

Regarding the allegation that Bomber Command never did anything to bring about the end of the war, that is absolute nonsense. Even Albert Speer is on record as saying that the efforts of Bomber Command constituted a second front for two years before D-Day. One only has to think of the massive resources that the Germans had to keep in the west to counter the efforts of the RAF: the large part of the *Luftwaffe*, the searchlights, the flak guns and the military personnel who could have been elsewhere. I hold the opinion that any activity in war, or even the threat of it, will occupy enemy forces that could otherwise be used. Consider the battleship *Tirpitz*, which spent the war in a Norwegian fiord and never fired a shot. By its mere presence it forced the Royal Navy to keep three battleships based in Scapa Flow doing nothing.

There is also the fact that the 88-millimetre Flak gun was a dual-purpose gun. It was also an anti-tank gun used on the battlefield to devastating effect on account of its extremely high muzzle velocity, needed to get its shells up to high altitudes. Any soldier who saw action in the Second World War will tell you of their fear of the 88 and its capabilities.

Rommel had twelve 88 anti-tank guns, which did terrible damage to British tanks because they could destroy our tanks at a range of a thousand yards, whereas we could not engage them over two hundred. If Rommel had had a lot of those, which were defending the *Reich*, Alamein might have had a different outcome.

I was also very lucky in being in two bomber squadrons that had very good post-war associations, 12 and 625. Unlike 12 Squadron, which had a history going back to the First World War, 625 Squadron only existed for a very short time. It was only formed in 1943 and was disbanded almost as soon as the war was over. As a result, the membership of the association was only very small. We had a reunion in a pub in London and a few more in Lincolnshire. But after about ten years it faded away.

In contrast, 12 Squadron had men who had been with them during its long life and has an association called the Wickenby Register, open to anybody who ever served in 12 Squadron or 626 Squadron, which was formed in 1943 by a flight from 12 Squadron and was based at Wickenby until it was disbanded when the war ended. There are still over a thousand members, including many who live in Australia.

One of the founder members was Arthur Lee who was the sole survivor when his Lancaster was shot down in a wood near the German town of Katzenellenbogen. (Yes, don't laugh, it's not by the sea. The name is the German for a cat's elbow

GROUNDED

and is situated on a sharp bend on a river.) Lee was captured in a very poor state of health resulting from the crash, but was not treated very well. He was put in a cell in the police station but only after the intervention of a soldier who happened to be at home on leave from the Russian front at the time. He drew his revolver and forced the mob, who were getting ready to lynch Arthur, to cease their activities and put him in the cell to await the arrival of the military to take him as a prisoner of war. There is no doubt that this action saved Arthur's life. When he returned home at the end of the war, Arthur often wondered who the unknown soldier had been, and wished that he could meet him and give him his heartfelt thanks.

Arthur then decided that it would be a good idea to form an association from ex-members of the squadron, and the Wickenby register was formed with him as member number one. The news soon spread by word of mouth and the membership rocketed. It was not long before I heard about it and my number is 440.

When I first came to a reunion it was at a hotel in Leicester where we had a dinner followed the next morning by a visit to Wickenby for a memorial service. One of the early projects was to have a memorial put up at Wickenby. This was done with a small memorial stone and a metal construction of 'Icarus falling' above it.

Now there happened a most extraordinary occurrence that has resulted in many members having some extremely happy experiences. It happened that the manager of the hotel was a German and when Arthur told him of his experiences in 1944, the manager told Arthur that he came from Katzenellenbogen and he would make enquiries the next time he went on leave. And, true enough, it was not long before he was able to tell Arthur that the man in question was Rudi Baltzer, a citizen of Katzenellenbogen who lived there now with a business in woodwork and carpentry. A visit by Arthur and he was able to meet his benefactor. They became instant friends and agreed also that war was a waste and a disaster and that forgiveness and conciliation was the way ahead.

Arthur had discovered that the German night fighters had an annual remembrance service at a memorial on the banks of the Rhine so he decided that it would be a good idea if he attended and laid a wreath from the RAF. It naturally caused a sensation when, after the German pilots had placed their wreaths, Arthur placed his own. After the service was over, contacts were made and friendships forged, which resulted in a series of visits between the Germans and the Wickenby Register.

The first one was when the German representatives came to a 12 Squadron reunion at RAF Binbrook. One of them was a general who turned out to be Hajo Hermann, the man who had formed the first unit with single-seaters in 1943, after the use of Window had caused the destruction of the Kammhuber Line, when the system of strict control of the fighters was replaced by one where they were to range away free. I also met another pilot, Martin Becker, who claimed to have shot down six Lancasters on the night of the raid on Nuremberg when we lost ninety-six planes. I remember that one of our party enquired if I would like to meet him. 'Will it worry you to meet somebody who has caused so much destruction to us?' I replied, 'No, they did it to us, we did it to them.' He was a charming man, a typical flying man who did what he had to do in the war to the best of his ability. He was exactly the same type of person as we meet in the RAF. We got on very well and I have a very nice autographed photograph of him that I value very much, although my son is not too keen about it.

As I had been attacked by a single-engined pilot in an Me109, when I spoke to Hajo Hermann, I told him about the attack and how amazed I had been to see my attacker. I said 'It wasn't you by any chance, was it?' He replied, 'No, certainly not.' I asked him why he could be so certain and he replied 'I would have gone up.'

Hermann has since written a book about his wartime experiences, written, naturally, in German but translated by Peter Hinchliffe, who was not a member of the Wickenby Register but who was a member of our party when we went on our journeys to Germany. When the book was printed in English under the title *Eagle's Wings* Peter very kindly was able to obtain a copy signed by Hermann, with the inscription 'To Squadron Leader Rowland with comradely greetings from Hajo Hermann', which I value very much.

Hermann had an amazing career in the war. He started off in the Spanish Civil War, flying three-engined Junkers 52. With the invasion of Poland he was flying Heinkel 111s, then after a spell attacking England he went to the Mediterranean flying Junkers 88s against Malta. This led to further action in these aircraft during the Greek campaign when his bombs scored a direct hit on a ship loaded with ammunition that exploded and destroyed half the port where it was moored, thus causing great difficulties to the British campaign.

He was then posted to flying a desk at headquarters in Berlin and it was while he was there that he had his plan to use day fighters at night. He put this to Goering who approved it and allowed him to form his own unit for the purpose. He flew many sorties with them and scored several victories. Later in the war he was in charge of the unit of German 'kamikazes' who collided with American bombers, though unlike their Japanese namesakes they did not all lose their lives. As the end of the war approached he had trained a unit to infiltrate Russian units and plant explosive devices, which did considerable damage. Several of his close subordinateshad been captured and the Russians announced two would be shot unless Hermann gave himself up. He did so, and was a prisoner of war for ten years. He was one of the last bunch to be released. He studied law and opened a legal practice in Dusseldorf from which he has now retired. He still holds the view that the Germans had been entitled to invade Poland. 'How would you have liked it if England had a corridor across the country from Liverpool to Lincoln that was ruled by a foreign power after the armistice of the first war?,' he says.

This was an extremely successful visit and it was agreed that next year a party from the Wickenby Register would visit them in Germany.

When the time came, a party of Wickenby Register members was formed. I put my name down and about a dozen went, including a few wives. We flew from Gatwick to Frankfurt by British Airways. We met each other in the airport and as we were not all acquainted with each other we all wore the new Wickenby Register tie, which proved very useful for identifying each other. A few days earlier there had been a report in the press about a British Airways plane, in which the windscreen had somehow become detached and the pilot had very nearly been sucked out through the hole. He had only been saved by the second pilot and the steward who had managed to pull him back to safety. As we walked out to the plane I saw the captain sitting at his cockpit window, so I called up to him 'I hope you've got the windscreen firmly fixed in place.' He grabbed hold if it, gave it a damn good shake and replied 'Yes, it's fastened on as tight as a drum,' and gave me a thumbs up sign out of the window. I'm happy to say that we had a trouble-free flight to Frankfurt where we were met by a few of our guests who had with them for our use a comfortable twenty-seater bus, which they told us was at our disposal for the duration of our stay.

Grounded

We were taken to Sobernheim, a *German* Air Force Base. I am not sure if that is the correct name or whether it is still called the *Luftwaffe*. Anyway, they are now our gallant and much valued and admired allies. We were taken to a large barrack block, unoccupied at the time, where we were given rooms, although those with wives were put up in a local hotel as being a little less spartan for the ladies. But the barrack block was very comfortable with plenty of baths and comfortable beds.

I shared a room with Eric Foinette who had been shot down in a Wellington in 1942 and had been a prisoner of war for several years until the end of the war. He had been much cleverer than many prisoners and had taken a course in civil engineering and obtained a good degree by post through the Red Cross. The result was that he had been able to get employment with one of the large engineering firms where he had had a successful career until he retired.

The next day, we attended a memorial service at one of the military memorials, which was attended by some German Air Force top brass where our presence was greeted with enthusiasm. After lunch we went to Katzenellenbogen and called at the house of Rudi Balzer, where we received a most enthusiastic welcome. We were extremely impressed with his house, which with the benefit of his carpentry business had been decorated in a most sumptuous way with large amounts of wood panelling.

After lunch we went up to the site in the woods above the town where Arthur's plane had crashed so many years ago. The site was kept apart by light fencing and it was decided that a wooden cross in memory would be erected to mark the spot. Rudi would make the cross and it would be engraved with the words 'Father forgive us' in English and German, in the spirit of conciliation and friendship that now existed between the British and German peoples.

That evening, we were to be entertained at a reunion celebration that was to be held in a large hangar up at the airfield. When we arrived and gathered at the door to enter we were asked to wait a few moments until the veterans were ready for our entry. When we finally entered, we discovered that we were to be treated as royal guests. The room was full of large tables, each with ten seats. With a head table raised a few feet along one side, there was an orchestra and as we entered and made our way to our seats, which had been kept for us on two of the tables, we received a standing ovation to the tune of 'Tipperary'. It was most moving and there was not a sign of any animosity at some of the people who had come to destroy their cities. We had a very enjoyable evening with plenty to drink and eat. We were all called up to the top table and introduced individually to the audience.

During the evening we were able to make the acquaintance of many of the German wartime fighter pilots, notably Hajo Hermann who came to our table and told us something of his experiences. Another I remember well was a Dr Ernst Holtschmit who I had the pleasure of meeting again at later reunions. He had been a pilot on Junkers 88s in Norway, attacking the British convoys taking supplies to the Russians at Murmansk. He had been one of those selected by General Hermann to fly the single-seater fighters at night in all weather. Needless to say, when Hermann chose his pilots to fly in such arduous conditions he went entirely to the bomber squadrons for his recruits.

Another one I spoke to was very puzzled about so many RAF aircraft flying together in close proximity. I explained to him that a bomber stream of six hundred planes passing over a target in half an hour at two hundred knots would be about a hundred miles long, which was only six planes to the mile. And they would not be all on railway lines but could be flying at any height between 18,000 and 22,000 feet and also at anything up to ten miles on either side of the intended track; they were not really that close together. They were a little closer together when they came to the target area but the risk here was reduced because there was a lot of light from the searchlights. When I explained this to him his face cleared and he said, 'Ah yes, I can see now what you mean.'

The following day we were taken to the town of Rudesheim on the Rhine, a centre of the wine trade, where we had the opportunity to taste the local vintages and order some if we wanted to. I think that most of us did; I know that I had half a dozen bottles. After that we boarded a river cruiser and took a short trip up the river to the town of Bacharach. The thought crossed my mind 'I wonder if Burt was born here?' but I decided probably not as I think he was American.

We returned to the hangar for lunch. A counter had been set up along one side of the room, which contained some huge tureens of soup and plates of thickly sliced black bread. I was served a big bowl of the soup and given a piece of the bread and I have to confess that the thought passed through my head that it looked rather a poor lunch and not very hospitable. It was a thick soup with lots of bits in it and I set about it with vigour as I was pretty hungry. I have never changed my mind about anything so quickly about anything. By the time I had finished it I felt as satisfied after a meal as I have ever been. I said to myself, 'If this is what the German Army get for lunch every day I'm not surprised they are so successful.'

That evening we had a smaller gathering with those of the fighter pilots who had come to England and then the following morning it was time to set off for home. After a leisurely breakfast we set off to catch our plane at midday. But the traffic was very heavy and it seemed as if we were not going to be there in time. When we reached the airport it was very nearly take-off time and we had to run to the check-in point, hoping we were not going to miss our connection. But to our relief we were told when we got there that the plane was only just landing on arrival and there was no hurry.

There has been a succession of these reunions since then. I went on a couple of them myself. But with the passing away of members it became difficult to make up the numbers so it was merged with the Doncaster Air Gunners Association. With their numbers dropping too, it has been carried on by the ladies, so the idea of peace and reconciliation is still going.

I was surprised one day to receive a request from Cranwell for me to let them have a photograph of me to hang in their hall of fame. I sent them a choice of several and they chose the picture of me standing by my Lysander at Old Sarum in March 1940. But I regret I have not been able to locate it since. Perhaps it has been shunted off to make way for other more eminent people. But it was an honour to be asked.

About twenty-nine years ago I also started going to meetings of the Old Cranwellian Association, which is held at Cranwell every summer, consisting of sporting events after lunch, followed by a dinner in the evening. There was a list of those attending on the notice board in order of attendance as flight cadets. When I first attended I was fairly well down the list, but as the years passed and time took its toll I gradually moved up the list until I was at the top and didn't really know anybody there, so I do not go anymore. But at the beginning it was very pleasant to meet some of the few survivors from the war. I used to shoot in the clay pigeon shooting competition. Another shooter was Jimmy Stack, a charming man who had won the Sword of Honour in the last term before the war and had a distinguished career, ending up as an Air Chief Marshal and president of the Old Cranwellian Association. Others I was delighted to see again were Peter Balean, now a retired squadron leader like me, who had been in the term before me, and John Sowrey, now a retired air commodore who had gone with me to 613 Squadron in 1940. Unfortunately, all these are now no longer with us and the numbers of pre-war cadets almost non-existent.

I remember one year we had a record attendance because Prince Charles was the guest of honour. I remember Douglas Bader was there. There was a bit of a hitch at dinner. The programme was for drinks in the rotunda at 7.30 pm and dinner at 8 pm. Prince Charles was flying up by helicopter from Buckingham Palace to arrive at about seven. Unfortunately, there was a very strong wind blowing straight from Cranwell to London, and with helicopters being very slow the flying time was much increased. We all waited in the rotunda, and waited, and waited. We obviously could not start without the guest of honour so we were about an hour and a half late before we got in to dinner. Nevertheless, the evening after dinner was as enjoyable as ever.

My last visit to Cranwell was a couple of years ago when I was invited as guest after dinner speaker at an end of course guest night.

I had an enjoyable experience a few years ago at the Lincoln Aviation Heritage Centre at East Kirkby. They have a Lancaster they call *Just Jane*. The Centre is situated on the site of a Second World War bomber base, and includes the old Second World War flying control building and a section of runway and perimeter track. They have managed at great expense to get all four engines running. On certain days they taxi the aircraft along the track. They carry twenty passengers whom they charge £160. This sounds a lot, but the costs of keeping the engines running are enormous.

A few years ago they ran a Heroes day where aircraft enthusiasts were invited to obtain signatures in their books, pictures, and papers from the twenty or so ex-aircrew who were seated at a number of tables. I was invited to take part in the signing, and in addition was given a ride in the taxi ride free of charge. I was absolutely amazed at the number of people who came. I must have given a couple of hundred signatures, mostly in the fly leaf of the book *Bomber Boys Fight Back*, which had just been published. My hand was quite sore by the time I had finished, but it was well worth it for the taxi ride in *Just Jane*. I am the proud possessor of a photograph taken by my eldest son of me looking out of the pilot's seat window. To see the engines started up and hear that well-known Merlin sound was fantastic and brought back many memories, nearly all pleasant.

Another strange experience was to be able to talk to Guy Gibson. Not the person himself, of course, as he was killed in 1944 in a Mosquito returning from a raid on Munchen Gladbach. But I spoke with Richard Todd, the actor who played his part in the film *The Dam Busters* so well. Like me, he is a lot older now but unlike me he was in a wheel chair, but very interesting to talk to. He had been roped in by the organizers to increase the attractions, though *Just Jane* was the star.

One way in which airline flying today differs from my day is in the cabin crew. When I started in BOAC there was no such thing. On the Dakotas there was a lunch box under the seat with a picnic lunch provided by the catering department. When I started on the horseshoe route via Lagos to Cairo, we had a steward but he had no galley. However, he had a space at the back of the passenger cabin where he had a box with a few necessities with which to minister to the needs of the crew and passengers. He would renew his stocks as we went along and at the end of the trip distributed a few well received goodies that he had left to the crew. When we got the Haltons we had a small galley and a steward, which was very welcome as the flights were a lot longer, up to eight hours, so that some refreshment was needed. One day I landed at Luqa and saw that the Dakotas now had stewardesses. And extremely attractive they were too. At that time the job as an airline stewardess was much sought after with the attraction of foreign travel.

But on the Yorks they still had stewards. When I was on the Accra run one day I found that I had a stewardess. There were a lot of British expats living in West Africa who had children at school in England. They used to fly out to West Africa for the holidays and when a bunch of these travelled out BOAC put a stewardess on board to look after them. The girl I took was a very charming lady; in fact, she was the sister-in-law of John Mills, the film actor, which goes to show the type of women attracted to the job in those days. The job is nothing like as worthwhile today as it was then.

The tragedy with the Comets was a disaster for BOAC. At a stroke, they lost the lead in the airline industry where they had hoped to be ahead of every other airline and had to see Boeing supply everybody, including themselves, with their 707. But they survived and, after amalgamating again with BEA to form British Airways, they are now one of the largest and most respected airlines in the world. My greatest regret is that they did it without me.

Return Flights in War and Peace

Index

Aberaeron, Cardigan 10
Accra 158, 162, 181, 182, 190, 191, 192
   sawmill 190-191
Africa, BOAC route to Cairo across 171-172, 173, 176-177, 178, 186
Africa, West, BOAC route through 157-158, 161, 162-163, 177-178, 181-182, 188-189, 207
Aikens, Flt Lt Frankie 64
air gunners 43
Air Ministry 60, 67
Air Transport Auxiliary (ATA) pilots 57, 130
airfield lights 83-85
Airspeed Ferry 11
Airspeed Oxford 23, 27, 29, 32, 76
Aldermaston aerodrome 179
Alvis open four-seater car 39
American Lancaster pilot 143-144
American soldiers 154-155
Amesbury 37
Amiens prison 19-20
And the Walls Came Tumbling Down 20
Anderson, Sqn Ldr (later Grp Capt) RF, DFC 41-42, 47, 48-49, 53
annuities 12-13
anti-aircraft fire (flak) 80, 117-118
Armstrong Whitworth Whitley 77
artillery spotting 45
ATA (Air Transport Auxiliary) pilots 57, 130
Atlantic, battle of the 24
Atlas Assurance Company 11-13, 14, 16
Augsburg, MAN U-boat engine factory raid 91-92
Austin Seven car 34, 38, 39
Avro
   504: 10-11
   Anson 57
   Lancaster 76, 85, 87, 88, 115, 119-120, 126, 129, 130-131, 145, 148, 162, 166
      autopilot 130-131
      ED359 120
      Merlin engines 104, 143, 206
      preserved (*Just Jane*) 205, 206
      W4990 (V Vic) 98-99, 101-102, 110, 119, 120, 148-149
   Tudor 162
   Tutor 20-21, 26, 29, 63, 72
   York 183, 207

Bacharach 203
Bader, Douglas 205
Baghdad 159
Bailey, Bill 151
Baldwin, AVM JEA 19, 27, 28
Balean, Peter 204-205
Baltzer, Rudi 197-198, 201
Barry, Glamorgan 113
Barthropp, P/O Paddy 47, 48
Basra 183
Bathurst 161, 181
BEA (British European Airways) 174, 207
Beachy Head 102, 115
Becker, Martin 198
Beecroft, Sgt 133
BEF (British Expeditionary Force) 47, 50, 52
Benes, Mr (Czech prime minister) 159
Bennett, AVM DCT 81-82, 161
Bennett, P/O 58
Berlin Airlift 162
Berlin raid 112
Binns, P/O 133, 146
Birchall, Sgt 120, 121, 122
blind flying panel, standard 29
BOAC (British Overseas Airways Corporation) 147, 179, 182, 193, 207
   cabin service 206-207
   contract 175, 189, 190-192, 193
   navigation school 180
   route across Africa to Cairo 171-172, 173, 176-177, 178, 186
   route through West Africa 157-158, 161, 162-163, 177-178, 181-182, 188-189, 207
   secondment 148, 149, 151-155, 156-170, 171-174, 175-178, 179-182, 183-184, 185-189
   service to Cairo 156-157, 158, 159, 160, 163-164, 165-166, 168
   service to Helsinki 160-161

Return Flights in War and Peace

service to India 163, 183
service to Lagos 156, 158, 161, 162-163
service to Lisbon 156
service to Stockholm 160
Bochum raid 116
Boeing 707: 207
Boeing Flying Fortress 62
Bomber Boys Fight Back 206
Booker, Flt Lt Sam 72
Booth, Flt Lt 114
Boozer radar receiver 104-105
Boyle, Sqn Ldr (later ACM) 22, 28, 60
Brabazon Commission 162
Bristol 16, 17, 151, 170
Bristol Airport (Lulsgate Bottom) 160
British Airways 200, 207
British European Airways (BEA) 174, 207
British Expeditionary Force (BEF) 47, 50, 52
British Overseas Airways Corporation *see* BOAC
British South American Airways (BSAA) 161-162
Brown, P/O Bernard 47-48, 58
Brown, Sgt Murray 93
Brunswick raid 145
BSAA (British South American Airways) 161-162
Burberry's 19

Cairo 168, 169, 172
  Almaza airport 156, 158, 159, 165, 172
  BOAC route across Africa to 171-172, 173, 176-177, 178, 186
  BOAC service to 156-157, 158, 159, 160, 163-164, 165-166, 168
  Gezirah club 173
  pyramids 172-173
Calais raids 47, 48-49, 50, 52, 53, 147
Calcutta 184-185
camp kit 57
Canadair Argonaut 193
Canadian Air Force, Royal: No. 1 Sqn 39
Carras, W/O 141-142
Casablanca 181
Castel Benito 156, 159, 186
Catania 165
Chandler (ex-Cranwell pilot) 45
'Channel Dash' 94-95
Charles, Prince 205
Charlie (Accra sawmill employee) 190-191
Clift, Flt Lt 156
Cobham, Alan, and Flying Circus 10, 11
Coles, Flight Cadet 24

Cologne raids 101, 102-103, 104
  first 1,000 bomber raid 77
compass, DR (Distant Reading) 88-89
Conacher, LAC (later Sgt) 43, 49, 58
Connelly, Wg Cdr 139
craps game 154-155
Craven, Wg Cdr 114
Crummy, Grp Capt 98
Currie, Sgt Jack 109, 147
Czechoslovakian government 159

D-Day operations 135
Dam Busters, The (film) 206
Davies, Sgt 133
de Havilland
  Comet 193, 194, 207
  DH60 Moth 14, 15
  DH88 Comet 167
  Dominie 76
  Mosquito 71, 82, 86, 97, 142
  Tiger Moth 16, 115
Desoutter biplane 10
Doncaster Air Gunners Association 204
Doncaster race course 30
Douglas
  Dakota 151, 152, 158, 159, 166-167, 169-170, 176, 179, 206, 207
  DC-2 167
  DC-3 167
  Havoc 75
Drem flare path 83-84
Duisberg raid 134
Dunkirk 47, 52
Dusseldorf raid 123
Dyas, Mr 12, 13

Eagle's Wings 199
East Kirkby airfield 205-206
Edmonds (613 Sqn pilot) 57-58
Edwards, Flt Sgt (later W/O) Charlie 87, 96, 106, 110, 112, 116-117
Edy, P/O Al, DFC 42, 47, 49, 53, 58
El Adem 156, 163, 166, 167
El Fasher 172, 177
Ellis, Sgt, CGM 116
Empire Training Scheme 64, 152-153
England to Australia air race (1934) 167
Ermine Street 23
Essen raid 106-107

Farhit family 176
fatigue, crew 157-158
Fishman, Jack 20

210

flak (anti-aircraft fire) 80, 117-118
Flak gun, 88mm 196
flare path, Drem 83-84
flying instruction 60-61, 62, 63, 149-150
'flying instructor's lament, The' (poem) 149
Foinette, Eric 201
formation flying 62
Foyles bookshop 169
Frankfurt 200
Frankfurt raid 118
Freetown 161, 171
French Resistance 20
French targets 123-124, 131, 134, 135-137, 141-143, 144, 146

Gambia 161
gambling 154-155, 187-188
Geddes, Flight Cadet 24
Gee navigational aid 85-86
Gelsenkirchen raids 97-100, 105-106
Genoa raid 110
German night fighters 80-81, 98, 103-104, 109-110, 118, 119-120, 127, 198, 199, 202
  annual remembrance service 198
Germany, Wickenby Register visit to 200-204
Gibson, Guy 206
Gibson, Capt 163, 183, 194
Gillingham, Kent 120
Gilze-Rijen airfield raid 146
Gironde river 100-101
Glamorgan County Council 11
Glasgow 134, 135
Gneisenau 94-95
gold cargo 165-166
Gold Coast 158, 162, 163
Gore, P/O 47, 49
Gort, Lord, VC 25
Gosport tubes 60-61, 85
Goule, Flt Lt Haydn 113, 123, 129
Guernica 195
Guille, Flight Cadet 24
gun, 88mm Flak 196

H2S radar aid 82, 145
Haddon, Capt 194
Hagen raid 116
Hague, The, *Gestapo* building 71
Haig, Wg Cdr Douglas 'Duggie' 132-133, 134, 135, 139, 147, 189
Hamble 16-17
Hamburg, battle of 107-109
Handley Page Halifax 88, 125, 126, 166
Handley Page Halton 179, 180, 181, 182, 206-207
Hanover raids 115-116, 118-119, 120, 121-123
Harris, ACM Arthur 'Bomber' 132, 195
Hawker
  Audax 34
  Hart 23, 26, 29, 31, 34, 52
  Hector 34-35, 38, 39, 41, 42, 46, 47-49, 50, 52, 53, 54, 147
    armament 47, 50-51
    K8108 49
    K8111 53-54
  Hind 16
  Horsley 10
  Hurricane 49, 65
    Mk 1: 68-69
Helsinki BOAC service 160-161
Hermann, Maj Hajo 110, 198-200, 202
Heyworth, Sqn Ldr, DFC 91, 92-93, 123
Hillary, Richard 65
Hinchcliffe, Peter 199
Hitler, Adolf 15, 22, 167, 195
Holmes, Wg Cdr 'Speedy' 60, 72, 75, 76
Holtschmit, Dr Ernst 202
Houghton, P/O 'Tiger' 36, 38, 42-43, 49, 57
Howard-Williams, Flight Cadet 33
Hunt, Sqn Ldr 159
Hurn Aerodrome 151, 156, 159, 169

Imperial Airways 30
India, BOAC service to 163, 183
India, hotels in 185
India during partition 183-184

Jacksons Faces 43-44
Jaques, Sgt 133
Jenkyn, P/O 49
jet aircraft 193-194
Jones, Cliff 24

Kammhuber Line 80-81, 109, 198
Kano 158, 171, 176, 181, 182, 189
Karachi 163, 183, 185
Katzenellenbogen 196-198, 201
Kennedy, Sgt Ken 79, 86, 105, 107, 122
Kermode, AC 21
Khartoum 172, 177
  dentist 178
  Grand Hotel 172
Kiel harbour, minelaying in 133
Kiel raids 142, 145
Kimpton, Flight Cadet 23
Kingston-upon-Thames 11-12
Klemm Swallow 55, 57

211

KLM 166-167
Knighton Down 46

Lagos, BOAC service to 156, 158, 161, 162-163
landing at night 83-85
landings 61-62
Last Enemy, The 65
Le Cupon raid 134
Le Havre raid 146-147
Lecky, Flight Cadet 30
Lee, Arthur 196-197, 198, 201
Lee, Sqn Ldr 39
Leicester, hotel 197
Les Landes raid 142
Leverkusen raid 112
Lewis, Capt 156
Lighton, P/O 91
lights, airfield 83-85
Lincoln 94, 135
Lincoln Aviation Heritage Centre 205-206
Lincolnshire aerodromes 84
Lines, F/O 14
Link Trainer 28, 29
Lisbon 173
   BOAC service to 156
Lockheed Constellation 179
London
   City of 11-12, 13
   Great Portland Street 13-14
   Kilburn 175
   Ruislip 175-176
   Sir John Cass Academy 13
   Streatham 14
London Airport (Heathrow) 170, 174, 176
London Welsh rugby team 24
Louth, Mason's Arms 135
low flying 96
Ludlow Hewitt, ACM Sir Edgar 47
Lunghi 171
Lyons, Sgt Pete 'Joe' 79-80, 89, 105, 106, 111-112, 115, 118, 119, 120, 148-149

Mablethorpe 99
Macdonald, Flt Lt, RAAF 21
Macey, Sgt 117
Macintyre, Wg Cdr 64, 89-90
Mahaddie, Flt Lt (later Grp Capt) 76-77
Mahmoud, Mr (Cairo customs officer) 168, 169
Maiduguri 171, 176-177
   leper colony, lady doctor 176-177
Mailly-le-Camp raid 131, 136, 137

malaria 162-163
Malta, Luqa airport 163, 207
MAN U-boat engine factory 91-92
Mannheim raid 111
Marrs, P/O 22, 33, 45
Marsh, P/O Marcus 36, 43
Marville raid 134
master bomber tactic 112, 136, 137
Mayger, Capt 171, 173
Mazaryk, Jan 159
McIndoe, Dr 65
McMichael, Section Officer Jean *see* Rowland, Jean
Mepacrine 162-163
Messerschmitt 109: 121, 198-199
Miles Magister 15, 16, 30
Miles Martinet 79-80
Miles Master 62, 63, 68, 69, 72, 73
Mills, John, sister-in-law of 207
minelaying (*Gardening*) operations 100-101, 133
Modane raid 123-124
Montrose 65, 66
Moore, Grace 166-167
Morgan, Flight Cadet Senior Under Officer RAG 24
Munchengladbach raid 114
Mundy, Flight Cadet Bob 31, 45
Munich raid 117
Munslow, Sqn Ldr 139, 141

NAAFI store 167-168
navigation exams 179-180
navigation system, Oboe 82-83, 142
navigational aid, Gee 85-86
Nescafé 182
Nettleton, Acting Sqn Ldr John Dering, VC 91-92
New Quay, Cardigan 10
night flying 30-31, 64-65, 67
Nile river 172, 173
Nixon-Smith, Gordon 13-14
Noden, Flt Lt Bob 88, 173-174
Noden, Jean 174
North American Mustang 71
North Sea coast 55-56
North West Building Society 175
Northolt Aerodrome 159
Nuremberg raids 109, 111, 114-115, 137, 198

Oboe navigation system 82-83, 142
Observer Corps 96
Oeuf raid 144

Old Cranwellian Association 204-205
Olley, Flt Lt 76
Operation *Jericho* 19-20

Paddy (Irish ACII at Wickenby) 91, 106
Parry, Flt Sgt Derrick 78-79, 86, 105, 107, 108, 112
Pauillac raid 142-144
Peenemunde raid 111-112
photography, aerial 38, 83, 146-147
Pickard, P/O (later Grp Capt, DSO** DFC) Percy 19-20
pilot training 60-61, 62, 63, 149-150
Pitlochry, farm near 168
Plumb, P/O 45
Police, Service 139
Polish pilots 67-68
Port Etienne 161
Porthcawl 10-11
Price-Stevens, Capt 161
Prioleau, Pete 71, 72, 75
Punch poem 149

Rabat 161
radar 85-86 *see also* Oboe navigation system
radar aid, H2S 82, 145
radar receiver, Boozer 104-105
radio communication 85
rainbow as complete circle 177-178
Rajpipla, Maharajah of 36
Randall, Sgt 118, 123
Remscheid raid 108
Resistance, French 20
Revell, Flt Lt 'Foxy' 20
Revigny raid 137-138, 139
Rheine-Salzbergen airfield raid 147
Risi, Flt Sgt 123
Robinson, Sgt 'Robbie' 86, 101, 111-112, 120-121, 122
Robotham, Sgt 133
Rommel, Erwin 196
Roosevelt, Franklin D 181
Rothwell, Flight Cadet 29-30
Rowland, David (brother) 13, 73-74, 113, 154, 175, 194
Rowland, Jean (wife) 72-73, 139, 148, 152, 174
  dog Bonnie 148
  and house improvements 189-190, 191-192
  marriage to John 134, 135
  mother 134, 135, 168
Rowland, John, father of 10, 11, 16, 20, 25, 39, 43, 113, 154

Rowland, John, mother of 15, 16, 17, 25, 43, 74, 86, 113, 154, 193
Rowland, Michael (son) 72
Rowland, Philip (son) 72
Royal Air Force
  Army Co-operation squadrons 41-42
    artillery spotting 45-46
  Bomber Command 80, 83, 94-95, 123, 127, 153, 154, 195
  Central Flying School (CFS), Upavon 60, 61, 63, 64, 71-72, 73, 74, 75-77, 84
  Daily Routine Orders (DROs) 27
  Empire Central Flying School (ECFS), Hullavington 77
  Flying Training Schools (FTS) 23, 26
  Lancaster Finishing School (LFS), No. 1: 100, 120, 147-149
  No. 1 Group 88
  No. 3 Group 19
    HQ, Newmarket 139, 148
  Pathfinder Force 81-82, 83, 97, 112, 114-115, 118, 136, 145
  School of Army Co-operation, Old Sarum 27, 33, 34, 35-40
    aerial photography 38
    car crash 38-39
    gas spraying training 37-38
    tactical exercises without troops (TEWTS) 36
  Training Command 80, 84, 85
  University Air Squadron pupils 23-24, 26, 27
Royal Air Force College, Cranwell 9, 15, 18-19, 20-25, 26-28, 29-32, 33, 75
  Advanced Training Squadron 29
  B Squadron 18
  battle flight 30
  cross-country flight 29-30
  'First Term Boxing' 21-22
  night circuits and landings 30-31
  at outbreak of war 26-27
  passing out parade 24, 25
  photography/practical joke by author 32
  reunions 204-205
  rugby team 23-24
  sport 21-22, 23-24
  talk by Wellington squadron commander 27-28
  warrant officer 9
Royal Air Force squadrons
  bomber, life on 93-94
  fighter, life on 95
  No. 12: 89, 90, 91, 92-94, 95-104, 105-109,

110-117, 118-119, 120-124, 196
　post-war association *see* Wickenby Register
　No. 44 (Rhodesia) 91-92
　No. 101: 88
　No. 111: 65
　No. 300: 89-90
　No. 460: 139-141
　No. 617: 141
　No. 625: 132, 133-139, 141-147, 196
　　post-war association 196
　　warrant officer 133
　No. 626: 196
Royal Air Force stations
　Andover 40
　Binbrook 57, 132, 139-141, 144, 198
　Castle Combe, No. 3 FIS 77
　Church Fenton, Night Fighter OTU 64
　Elsham Wolds 88
　Faldingworth 96
　Filton 152
　Finningley 55, 56
　Firbeck 58, 59, 71
　Grangemouth, OTU 69
　Hawkinge 46, 47, 48, 49-50, 52
　Hemswell, Lancaster Finishing School 100, 120, 147-149
　Hixon, No. 30 OTU 78-80, 83, 85, 86
　Hullavington, Empire Central Flying School 77
　Kelstern 138, 139
　Leconfield 30
　Lindholme
　　1656 HCU 86, 87-88, 89-90, 124, 125-129, 130, 131
　　wing commander 129-130, 131
　Mildenhall 138
　Montrose 65-66, 95
　　Flying Training School 64, 65, 66-67, 68-70, 71
　Netherthorpe 55, 56-59
　Newmarket 148
　Odiham 40, 48, 52, 54
　Old Sarum *see* Royal Air Force: School of Army Co-operation
　Redhill, E&RFTS 14-15
　Renfrew 135
　St Athan 74, 86-87
　Upavon, CFS 60, 61, 63, 64, 71-72, 73, 74, 75-77, 84
　Warmwell 74
　Watchfield 152, 153
　West Freugh, armament camp 32-33
　Whitchurch, No. 33 E&RFTS 16, 17 *see also* Whitchurch Aerodrome
　Wickenby 84, 91, 93-94, 105, 106, 119, 120, 122, 132, 174, 196, 197
　Wittering 115
Royal Air Force Volunteer Reserve 14-15, 16-17, 41
Royal Auxiliary Air Force, No. 613 (City of Manchester) Sqn 35, 40, 41-44, 45-50, 52-54, 55-59, 71
Royal Navy 196
Rudesheim 203

Sahara desert 181-182, 188-189
Saint Elmo's Fire 164-165
Salisbury 38
Salisbury Plain 37, 46
Salmon, Capt 156
Salter, Wg Cdr 76
salutes 31
Sandhurst 15, 16, 28
Sandra lights 84
Sannerville raid 141
Scapa Flow 196
Scharnhorst 94-95
Schneider Trophy races 9-10
Schräge Musik night fighters 110, 118
searchlights, Sandra 84
Sharjah 163
sheikhs as passengers 177
Short, Sgt 89
Short Stirling 108
Skegness pier 96
Slater, Flt Lt (later Sqn Ldr) 20, 23, 31, 64, 71, 75-76
Sleaford station 9
Smirke, Charles 36
Smith, Flight Cadet 18-19, 30, 31
smuggling 169-170, 173
Snell, P/O Wally 91, 96, 115
Sobernheim air base 201, 202-203
Solbe, Flt Lt 31
Sowrey, Air Cdre John 40, 42, 57, 205
Spanish Civil War 195
Speer, Albert 195
Sperry (Link Trainer and gyro developer) 28
Stack, ACM Jimmy 204
Stack, Under Officer Cadet Neville 24
Stainer, W/Op Eddie 79
Stalag Luft III 36
Stettin raid 145-146
stewardesses 207
Stewart, P/O 21, 23, 31, 42, 47, 49

Stockholm BOAC service 160
Stonehenge 37
Stranraer 32-33
Stuttgart 142
Supermarine Spitfire 69, 130, 149, 159
Sweden 145-146
Switon, Sgt 67

Takoradi 162, 181
Target for Tonight (film) 19
Target Indicators (TIs) 82, 97
Tehran 159-160
Thompson, Sqn Ldr 14-15
thunderstorms, flying in 164-165, 177-178, 193-194
Times, The 57, 125
Tirpitz 195-196
Tobruk 167-168
Todd, Richard 206
Towle, Wg Cdr 113-114
Travis, P/O 133
Trenchard, AM Lord 39-40
Tripoli 181, 186-188 *see also* Castel Benito
   Albergo del Mehari (hotel) 186-187
   beaches 187-188
   harbour 187, 188
Tudge, P/O 39

V-1 flying bomb ('Doodlebug') targets 135, 141, 142, 144
Varley, Flt Lt Ginger 72
VD among aircrew 89

Vickers machine guns 47, 50-51
Vickers Wellington 78, 80
Vierzon raid 135, 136-137
Vire raid 135
Vizernes raid 141-142

Waghorn, Flt Lt 9-10
Waldron, P/O Frank 27-28
Watchfield, mother and daughter in 153-154
Watkyn, P/O 52
Wells, Flt Sgt 97, 100
West, Flt Lt 'Knocker' 72
Westbury-on-Trym 173-174, 175
Westland Lysander 34, 35-36, 38, 41, 45, 46, 49-50, 53, 54, 57-58, 71
Weston, Flt Lt Gus 42, 49, 56
Weston-super-Mare 11, 16, 43-44
Whitchurch Aerodrome 16, 17, 151, 156, 160, 176
Wickenby Register (No.12 Sqn association) 196, 197, 198, 200-204
Wilde Sau (Wild Boar) night fighter system 109
Wills family 174-175
Window device 107, 109, 198
Windsor Castle 146
Windsor Lad (horse) 36
Woods, Wg Cdr, DSO 91, 113-114
Woolwich 15, 16
World War II, start of 26
Wray, Air Cdre 144
Wyziekerski, Capt 160

215

Return Flights in War and Peace